POSSESSION and DESIRE
Working with addiction, compulsion, and dependency

Wayfinder Press
London, England

Copyright © 2012 Philip Harland
All rights reserved

ISBN 978-0-9561607-2-0

The right of Philip Harland to be identified as the author and illustrator of this work has been asserted in accordance with the UK Copyright, Designs, and Patents Act 1988

With the exception of brief quotations, no part of this publication may be reproduced or transmitted in any form or by any means without the permission in writing of the copyright holder and publisher

All enquiries to info@wayfinderpress.co.uk

*Choosing the temporary discomforts of desire
over the permanent discomforts of possession*

Contents

INTRODUCTION
Possession is one with Loss   7

PART I
VIOLENT PLEASURES
ARE RELIEFS OF PAIN   10
Understanding Addiction   10
An Exercise in Understanding   12
Patterns, Presuppositions, Power   13
Systemic Dependencies   13
The Act does not serve the Intent   15

PART II
SOME ADDICTIONS FEEL PHYSICAL
BUT ALL ADDICTIONS ARE MENTAL
A Model of Addiction   17
stage 1   Once upon a time   18
stage 2   Another time   19
stage 3   The next time   21
stage 4   Subsequently   22
stage 5   Eventually   23
stage 6   Finally   24
Applying the Model   24
Conclusion   25

PART III
THE PHYSICIAN'S PROVIDER   26
The Therapist Prepares   26
Addiction to Helping   27
Therapist Prejudice   28
Therapist Ethics   30
(Un)conscious Outcomes   31

PART IV
LIMIT OF DESIRES   33
Client Issues   33
Desire – Need – Possession   35
Client Presentations   37
I can take it or leave it   37
I can stop any time I want   38
I'm not hooked, you know   38
I can't give up and I must give up   39

PART V
RESOLVING ADDICTIVE
CONTRADICTIONS   41
Admitting Third Options   43
Negotiating   44
Escaping   45
Counter Double-Binding   47
Changing the Rules   48
Metaphor Modelling   49
Converging   50
Allowing   51

PART VI
AUDITING FOR X   53
Information Activating and Change
Questionnaire   55
Person   55
Possession   58
Pattern   60
Preference   63

Author and Acknowledgments   65
References and Further Reading   65
Self-Help Groups   65
Checklist for Change   67

POSSESSION and DESIRE

Working with addiction, compulsion and dependency ('X')

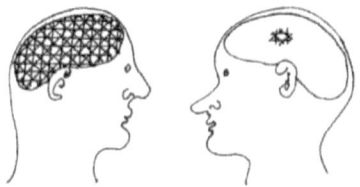

X = alcohol, anger, approval, caffeine, chocolate, cleaning, control, diets, drugs, eating, gambling, helping, indebtedness, power, relationship, religion, romance, self-harm, sex, shopping, smoking, therapy, video games, weight loss, etc., etc.

Introduction

Possession is one with Loss.
Dante, The Divine Comedy

It's not cool to be an addict. At best, you are a nuisance. At worst, it will kill you.

As a psychotherapist, I used to be uncertain about working with addictions. Too much had been written about them. There were too many kinds. As an ex-addict, I knew something (though not enough) of my own addictive patterns, and something (often too much) of those of my family, friends, colleagues, and clients, yet little to link them had emerged.

I was in a tangle, a muddle, a maze – exactly the sort of metaphor that my addictive clients would come up with to describe themselves. Experience and research have helped me exorcise my addictive ghosts. It aided my approach to the subject to realize that dependency sufferers had other problems too. A gambler client had a low anger threshold. A chocolate addict suffered from dyslexia. A lifetime smoker had high levels of anxiety. The other problem can be a way into working with the addiction and the addiction can be a way into working with the other problem. Where once I had thought of addiction as esoteric (having discounted my own history), I now saw it as ordinary.

I shall not be considering particular addictions in this paper, though several will get a mention here and there, but the addictive process. I shall deconstruct the way addictions, compulsions, and dependencies happen and suggest ways of doing something about them. By 'deconstruct' I mean separate out mental confusion. My Uncle Len had a reputation for fixing things – steam irons, vacuum cleaners, that kind of thing. He confided in me that it was no great skill. He simply took things apart and remembered where the screws went. This guide is more or less about that. It aims to dispel some of the misunderstandings and mystique around the addictive process and to offer a systematic approach to working with any of its multifarious forms and at any of its many levels, from the apparently harmless to the destructively complex.

Part I (VIOLENT PLEASURES ARE RELIEFS OF PAIN) identifies addiction as one of the unhappy consequences of the primal human wound: the fear of non-being. Part I is about understanding why this is so. It refers to neurophysiological research by scientists such as Gerald Edelman, but also to opinion and speculation of my own, so it is only fair that you know where that comes from. Part I will have more to say about my own addictions.

Part II (SOME ADDICTIONS FEEL PHYSICAL, BUT ALL ADDICTIONS ARE MENTAL) offers a six-stage model of addiction that breaks down what happens into its constituent parts. Addiction is a concept, a subject for study, but addicting is an activity; it is something we do. Part II takes the reader through the bodymind process of becoming addicted.

Part III (THE PHYSICIAN'S PROVIDER) considers therapist issues around the subject. It sorts some ideas about meaning and language in the assumptions we make. How does language affect our beliefs and practices? We look at the dangers of labelling and considers the difference between interfering and intervening in client process. The hidden snares of working with addiction are exposed. How do therapists get addicted to helping? How may we get unaddicted?

Part IV (LIMIT OF DESIRES) reflects on client issues. If addicting is an activity, then it involves choice. Addiction is not something we catch unwittingly, like flu. And as choice is centred in the individual, addicting and unaddicting is different for everyone. Part IV examines what clients say about themselves. The differences between wishing to 'quit' or 'control' are identified. The dangers of progression from simple desire to complex need to total possession are defined.

Part V (RESOLVING ADDICTIVE CONTRADICTIONS) deconstructs double-binds and dualities, including the familiar dilemma of being caught between aversion ('I must give up X') and attraction ('I can't give up X'). A number of approaches to resolving duality and contradictory thinking are to be found here: admitting third options, negotiating, escaping, counter double-binding, changing the rules, metaphor modelling, converging, and allowing.

Part VI (AUDITING FOR X) suggests a systematic way for facilitators of all kinds, including self-helpers, to work successfully with addictions, compulsions, and dependencies in any of their many forms. If all addictions are mental, they can be accessed, explored, and transformed neurolinguistically – that is, through language, metaphor, and self-modelling – as a more ecological alternative to medical means. Part VI unscrambles approaches to client assessment and offers a comprehensive information activating and change model applicable to any addictive behaviour.

"Whenever I see a new client," says psychotherapist Pamela Gawler-Wright, "I presuppose that change of some sort is already happening, otherwise unless they've been dragged along by a friend or relative, why are they here?" Most of us can learn to move from addictive state to non-addictive state without crossing too many frontiers in-between, but addiction is immense and untamed territory, with no single map and no easy passage. Anyone uncertain about which path to take will find the aids to navigation here useful both theoretically and practically. We may all look to the day when we can live with the occasional discomforts of desire without succumbing to the permanent discomforts of possession.

▶

Part I
Violent Pleasures are Reliefs of Pain
Plato, The Republic

Most of the research I have come across agrees that whatever other factors may be involved, addictions are desperate strategies aimed at warding off the terror of non-existence and its traumatic recursions and repercussions. Even the everyday compulsions and dependencies that most of us are familiar with are likely to relate to a fear of extinction brought on by an experience of deprivation, abuse, or upheaval, often in early childhood. We have only to witness the mind-numbing bewilderment on the face of a young girl caught on camera during the sinking of the cruise ship Concordia in February 2012 to know that trauma may appear at any age and in many forms.

My aim here to dispel some of the mystique around the addictive process, whether you happen to suffer yourself or claim never to have suffered. Politicians and commentators who make such a fuss about smoking, binge drinking, and drug taking in others might reflect on their reluctance to admit to a multitude of less conspicuous behavioural and systemic dependencies in themselves. Addiction is an unexceptional state.

Understanding Addiction

Every one of us is prone to suffer to a greater or lesser degree. One piece of research suggests that addiction is an attempt to compensate for inadequate breast-feeding. If as babies we learn that the world is not bountiful, as adults we will go out of our way to seek gratification. An alternative theory suggests that, on the contrary, addiction aims to reinstate abundant breast-feeding: instant gratification is our child/adult's inalienable right. Either way, few of us have scruples about pursuing or accepting whatever gratification the world can provide.

If the fact of addicting gives us something in common, there is more that makes us unique. And just as there is no one way of working with those other grand nominalizations[1] 'guilt', 'fear', and 'depression', there is no one way of working with addiction. There is, as I will show in Part II, an underlying structure to the addictive process, but approaches to treatment and recovery emerge from considering the needs and patterns of individuals.

For my own part, in my twenties and thirties I was on a search for the perfect relationship. I didn't think of it as an addiction. I didn't think much about it at all, but truth to tell these were desperate pleasures. If I stopped for a moment to think about how often and readily I fell in and out of love and desire, I would excuse myself as a victim – of circumstance, inheritance, and so on. In fact, I was an active volunteer. No-one was making these choices for me. Unfortunately, they didn't feel like choices. I was in the grip of a compulsion.

In my thirties, I read all I could about the psychology of pursuit and possession, and the existential void they were attempting to fill. And I began to see my unproductive patterns more plainly. "A relationship addict can become just as insane as an alcoholic," Anne Wilson Schaef points out in Beyond Therapy, Beyond Science. "It's the same disease." Schaef was making a systemic point. Therapists with an addiction to helping can hinder their clients' recovery. Dictators with an addiction to power can wipe out whole populations. My patterns were little different in principle to the unsociable habits of psychopaths, my father's pernicious addiction to nicotine, and any number of my relatives', friends', and colleagues' compulsive anger, drinking, gambling, or consumption of chocolate.

What lay behind my dependency? Crucial to my understanding was an early experience of what I can only describe as annihilation. When I was a child, my mother left my father, my sister, and myself to go a long way away and marry someone else. I had no warning. I fell into a void. I know it now as the dread of non-being that all trauma victims share. This is not a fear of death. It is worse. Alcoholics and drug addicts prove time and again that pain or life-threatening illness is not enough to deter them. What drives them is something darker than death – an intimation of the extinction of the self while alive: overwhelming feelings, expressed or repressed, of abandonment, powerlessness, worthlessness, insignificance.[2]

Like many such victims, I was caught in a vortex from which there was no escape. In this scenario, addicting is a predictable response to the spectre of isolation and alienation that haunts the human condition. It begins simply as a means of seeking a compensatory positive experience. The effects manifest in psychopathological patterns unique to every individual, but we can generalize: early abandonment may prompt a compulsive search for belonging; powerlessness to the pursuit of power through alcohol or the control of others; worthlessness to a quest for self-acceptance through sex; and so on. Addictive behaviour, like abusive behaviour, is a balm for the primal wound caused by the neglect or abuse, intentional or otherwise, of those with dominion over us,

An Exercise in Understanding

You will be relieved to know that you don't need to experience annihilation directly to understand the deeper reaches of addiction. Most of us possess a prerequisite for understanding: the desire for experience. Experimenting with drugs, for example, can lead to a habit, a habit to a compulsion. "The reality of any experimentation," said Blur singer Damon Albarn in a recent interview. "is that it can become habitual, and it can take over your life."

Think of a time when you were in thrall to some substance, behaviour, or belief that you found difficult to control, even if it was against your will or better judgement. An attachment to dieting, perhaps; an extra drink in the evening; an unthinking deference to teachers or priests; your lifetime collection of licence plate numbers; some minor indulgence that you never liked owning up to, but which gave you – it may give you still – a feeling of ownership, entitlement, a sense that you deserve its modest rewards.

Reflect for a moment on this presumption of entitlement. It may relate to something unresolved in your life: an experience of deprivation or coercion as a child; growing up in a dysfunctional family; or being sent to a school where you were taught to distance yourself from others instead of relating authentically. If you joined the healing or helping professions as a result of an early experience of separation or oppression, you will probably know quite a bit about the roots of your particular dependency.

For now, though, it's not necessary to know how it came about. Just recall any negative feelings you experienced around your attachment or indulgence – intimations of shame or anxiety, guilt, vulnerability. Whether the symptoms were mild or severe, imagine how any of them taken to extreme could have led you – perhaps they did – to the pit of despair. And deeper, darker yet, could have led to your self-destruction. You may now have a glimmer of understanding of the death of self and extinction of choice that characterize the later stages of addiction.

Patterns, Presuppositions, Power

In my own case, I stopped short, just, of self-destruction. Later, much later, I gave up on the no-longer-sustainable belief that I could sort things out unaided and went into personal therapy. And life began to change. At the risk of sounding unfair to those who go through mental turmoil in their therapy, I have to say I enjoyed every moment. It may have helped to have read so much psychology and philosophy first. That, and having a relentlessly positive view of the universe.

I got so far into the art and science of facilitating knowledge and healing that I went on to train as a therapist myself. I worked for a while in the conventional methodologies – analytic, humanistic, cognitive-behavioural, neurolinguistic – but felt far from comfortable. They were too interpretative. They could be exploitative. I wanted to work in a way that deferred to the real expertise of the client rather than to the imagined objectivity of the therapist. This led me before long to David Grove and the innovative practice of facilitating clients 'cleanly'.[3] The philosophical underpinnings of Clean Language and Clean Space, no less than their simple and respectful practices, perfectly matched my beliefs and values about the ethics and politics of change.[4] What is more, they worked. The evidence from clients was unambiguous.

Systemic Dependencies

Around this time, I realized that addiction is not only about individuals, but about society. We learn dependent and co-dependent behaviour from an early age. Any one of our everyday addictions – to drugs, sex, gambling, etc. – is a metaphor for our primary addiction to structures of authority, conformity, and sovereignty in our lives which curb self-determination and foster dependency.

Health professionals are not immune to the dependency disease. Although the stated aim of most therapists, medics, and agents of change is to support their clients and patients to be and heal themselves, it is much easier in practice to sustain them in the belief that recovery is a matter of conforming to the suggestions, instructions, and expectations of others. Just as the human instincts for community and spirituality were codified into the conventions and canons of organized religion, we have allowed our empathic instincts to be channelled into certified procedures and accredited institutions that give therapists what Schaef ("a recovering psychotherapist", as she calls herself) describes as "the illusion of control and the myth of objectivity."

The odd thing is that in this era of the search for a unity of science and healing, we should be seeking to reinforce archaic structures of control. It can only serve to codify the imbalance of power that exists between therapists and their clients. Institutionalizing the human potential movement is an oxymoron – a contradiction in terms that (literally) points to its own foolishness.

That, then, is the political context of this paper. When I use the word 'addiction', I shall be alluding not only to the usual suspects under the opening title, but also to the systemic dependencies that permeate our lives and hold us unknowingly hostage. When I use the word 'therapy', I wish to discriminate between traditional psychotherapy, the effect of which has been to cultivate a co-dependent relationship with the client through the use of interpretation, suggestion, and the illusion of therapist omnipotence – thereby reinforcing systemic dependency – and postmodern psychotherapy, which aims to facilitate self-authentic change and is, I believe, an instrument for the transformation of society. And when I use the word 'client' or 'patient', I mean you. Me. All who wish to free themselves to be no more or less than themselves.

We can note how patient/therapist co-dependence – a sub-system of systemic dependency – mirrors victim/rescuer, addict/supporter, and individual/institutional co-dependencies. Here is playwright Biljana Srbljanovic writing in 1999 about the failings of herself and her fellow citizens during the Balkan wars:

> *I ought to have done so much more. And what about those who didn't even do that? Those who called out the name of the president with erotic passion, who slobbered over his photographs as if they were icons, who were obedient and tame victims, but also brutal hangmen? Right now we need self-knowledge and Serbian denazification otherwise we are doomed forever.*

Each partner to such a co-dependency, whether victim or hangman, believes that the presence and actions of the other justify their own. Slobodan Milosevic plays persecutor to victim Serbs, who persecute dissident Kosovans, who became victims in turn.

victim-persecutor co-dependency

At which point Nato steps in to play rescuer to victim Kosovans and in so doing becomes persecutor to persecutor Serbs, who now become victims.

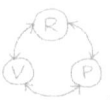

victim-persecutor-rescuer co-dependency

The result is a self-reinforcing cycle of co-dependency. Are we doomed forever? As therapists, we might protest that we are doing our best in a system that is far from evil, that in any case is one we inherited and do not have the power to change. Victim-speak. In fact, we lend energy to a society that encourages us to play victim, persecutor, and rescuer in turn.

> Victim–speak: 'I'm doing my best in the circumstances.'
> Persecutor–speak: 'You have problems.'
> Rescuer–speak: 'I come as expert with knowledge you do not have.'

Thus do systemic dependencies perpetuate. A Balkan dictator may have been a convenient deflector for our worst projections of ourselves, but we cannot escape our personal, internal responsibility for sustaining institutions and attitudes that maintain and extend these needless dyads and triads of co-dependency.[5]

The Act does not serve the Intent

It helped my understanding of systemic dependency to acknowledge that addiction correlates with abuse. Addictive behaviour is abusive behaviour. Abuse may not be the aim, but therein lays addiction's 'double dysfunction': the act does not serve the intent. The intention is to relieve pain, but the effect is to generate pain. This corrupts the victims and also those who support them, who become victims in turn. At its mildest, it may only mean that the addict is a source of irritation on occasion. At its worst, addicting gathers despair and degradation around it and ends in death.

What is it that links and encompasses each of these extremes and every degree in between? What is the addictive process and how does it work?

▸

Notes to Part I

1 *Nominalizations*: conceptual nouns such as 'addiction', 'fear', and 'depression' usually describe stuck states. Opening them up into verbs or activities can help mobilize stuckness. How do you *do* addiction, fear, depression?

2 *Annihilation*. In physics, it's what happens when a particle meets an anti-particle. The result is not 'nothing', but a different kind of energy. A proton encountering an anti-proton will turn into a number of unstable mesons which fly off from the annihilation point. That is a metaphor I can identify with. In psychological trauma, the annihilation 'energy' that results from a threat to psychic survival has been called 'unthinkable anxiety', 'disintegration anxiety', or 'nameless dread'.

3 *Clean Language, Clean Space, and Therapeutic Metaphor*: the therapist facilitates the client to transform their problem through verbal or nonverbal language without external interpretation or suggestion. Client metaphor is frequently the vehicle for exploration and discovery at the frontier between the conscious and unconscious mind. See cleanlanguage.co.uk and wayfinderpress.co.uk.

4 *Ethics and politics of change*: for more on the subject, read Part I of *Trust Me I'm The Patient: Clean Language, Metaphor, and the New Psychology of Change* and the article *Ethics, Love, and Power Relations* (both Wayfinder 2012).

5 *Victim-rescuer co-dependency*: even to believe there is some kind of intentionality to life – a force holding and directing us as evolution unfolds – seems to me to keep us in victim-rescuer mode: another node in our extensive network of systemic dependencies.

Part II
Some Addictions Feel Physical, But All Addictions Are Mental

Addiction is not a disease that we catch unwittingly or randomly, like flu or cancer. It is a behaviour and as such it involves choice. And as choice is centred in the individual, addicting and unaddicting are different for everyone. The addiction does not in itself define the addictive individual.

A Model of Addiction

The line between psychological dependency and what was once called physical addiction is now so blurred as to be indiscernible. The model of addiction here aims to show how that comes to be. We consider the brain mechanisms that underlie how we think, feel, remember, and act, and the role of both the unconscious and conscious mind in the addictive process. My evidence for the model stems from late 20th and early 21st century discoveries in neurobiology and evolutionary psychology. Particular credit goes to neuroscientist Gerald Edelman for linking the realms of neurology and psychology in a way that Freud could only dream of.

I have divided the addictive process into six stages: Once Upon a Time, Another Time, The Next Time, Subsequently, Eventually, and Finally. When you know at what stage you are personally with X, you will hopefully be able to work out how you got there as a basis for deciding where you wish to go next. How did the related behaviours originate? What possibilities for control did you have at the time you may have been out of control? What intimations of control do you have now for the future?

As we go through this model, I ask you to keep three things in mind.

> 1 We will probably never know everything about the way the mind works. Although all our mental awarenesses (thoughts, feelings, memories, etc.) are the evolutionary outcome of physical (neurophysiological) processes in the brain, they are not open to deconstruction in any simple sense. It is a fact that the brain is capable of many more combinations of connection than there are

particles in the universe (many millions more when I last counted), and just as the flavour of a stew is more than the sum of its ingredients, our thoughts, feelings, consciousness, sense of selfhood, etc., are complex emergent properties of our neural capacities. Precisely how this happens we may never fully know.

2 The model is necessarily crude. There are subtle differences between any model of human experience and the real thing.

3 When I refer to mind or body, I usually mean 'bodymind'. Whether the mind knows it all or whether the body knows things that the mind does not, is not very relevant here. All you need bear in mind (and body) is that the mind needs all the other organs of the body, including the brain, for full information.

Stage 1 Once Upon a Time

There is an external event. It could be, but does not have to be, single, sudden, or evidently traumatic, like falling off a cliff. It could be a pattern of sub-traumatic disturbance that extends over years – low-level violence, constant carping, the exercise of arbitrary power, etc. The brain itself does not 'see', 'hear', or 'feel' this event or events; the body experiences an onslaught of stimuli from the senses and constructs a symbolic representation in the physical space of the brain. And because every brain is a unique configuration of neuronal groupings with idiosyncratic synaptic and chemical connections, this particular brain, let us call it Alex's, makes a subjective interpretation of the stimuli, prompting

a bad feeling

A series of neural connections resulting in an uncomfortable or unpleasant internal sensation experienced by Alex somewhere in the body (usually gut, head, or heart). Alex may interpret it as anything from mild anxiety to utter hopelessness. An emotion is arguably the most complex of all mental states, commingled as it is with every other mental process (attention, memory, consciousness, etc.), and having its own individual, biographical, historical, and cultural connectors.

It is possible to deconstruct Alex's bad feeling, or 'negative-impact emotion', further as:

bad feeling = bodily sensation + judgement

Judgement is an idiosyncratic neural interaction arising from Alex's emotional history. It gives a 'weighting' or 'value' to the event. Alex's bad feeling will probably be worse if the judgement includes a belief that the event is unjust or that there is negative intentionality behind it. The combination of

event + sensation + judgement = bad feeling

is experienced by Alex as a single impactful event and leaves a 'wound'.

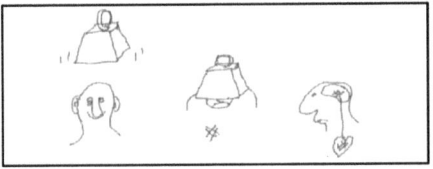

external event   bad feeling   bodymind wound

Stage 1 Once upon a time

The wound is not a faithful reflection of the event, but a subjectively constructed memory circuit, affirmed or repressed at the time by other parts of Alex's brain. Nerve cell signals may be excitatory or inhibitory, and it is their complex interactivity – there can be up to 100,000 individual synaptic connections *per cell* – which determines what kind of signal is ultimately received by other cells. So delicate is the balance that it sometimes seems almost arbitrary whether Alex's wound remains raw or is partly healed, whether it is obvious or not at any given time, whether it flares easily or is heavily insulated.

Stage 2 Another Time

Another key event occurs – a new thought or feeling, a remembered thought or feeling, or a response to another event. This event has a particular impact on Alex. Some research suggests that it is likely to occur in adolescence, when there is radical disturbance generally, but it can happen at any time. The event produces a new neural sequence, which triggers

a bad feeling in Alex *similar* to the original bad feeling

Reminding Alex's brain, consciously or not, of the original event–value judgment and evoking *a memory of the wound*

This reconstruction of the original memory may be identified consciously or not by Alex.

So far, so normal. In a personal history of addiction, however, another significant event occurs around this time:

doing X – smoking, drinking, sex, etc.

An activity that has associations with positive benefit: assertion-of-self-against-authority, socialising-with-peers, reward-for-bad-experience, novel-pleasure, and so on. Many alcoholics remember their first drinking experience in great detail. Compulsive gamblers may have a significant win at an early time in their lives. Nicotine, heroin, or cocaine entering the bloodstream triggers the release of dopamine, a neuro-transmitter associated with feelings of pleasure. Chocolate gives fast-injection energy from sugar and caffeine and mood enhancement from phenyl-ethylamine and theo-bromine. Caffeine stimulates the heart by suppressing the effects of adenosine, one of the brain's naturally inhibitory chemicals, which produces a perking effect.

The effect of doing X is to

feel good

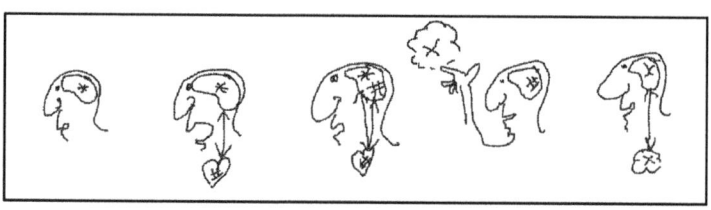

new event in brain   bad feeling   memory of wound   do X   feel good

Stage 2 Another time

The good feeling establishes another neural circuit, which has synaptic connections to the concurrent (active at the same time) 'doing X' circuit, which itself has synaptic connections to the contemporaneous (active in the same period of time) 'bad feeling' circuit, which in turn has synaptic connections to the primary (original) 'bad feeling' circuit.

A neural sequence of association from 'bad feeling' to 'good feeling' is thus formed and learned. Addiction is not necessarily a one-time learning, but a learning over time.

Stage 3 The Next Time

There is another, *similar*, event in the brain, which triggers

> another *similar* bad feeling

Now something new happens. The ready-formed neural pattern of association, consisting of Alex's old bad feeling circuit, the doing X circuit and the feeling-better circuit, is triggered *as one event*. And so immediate is the association that Alex's mind finds it impossible to separate out its constituent parts in order to know what is really happening. The result is an exceptionally intense, self-generated, hallucinatory experience interpreted by Alex as a 'craving', or a

> desire for X in order to feel better

which is followed by

> doing X

resulting in another

> good feeling

which evolves into a higher-order feeling of apparent

> satisfaction

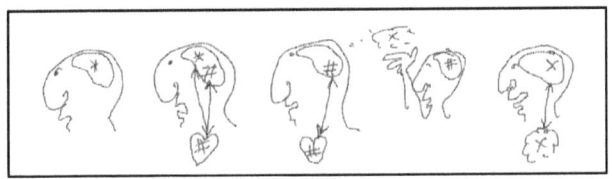

similar event   similar feeling   desire for X   do X, feel better   satisfaction

Stage 3 The next time

Satisfaction is the feeling that comes from having done something to solve a problem – in this case, wanting to lose a bad feeling. The satisfaction is self-deceiving. It is based on the perception that X solved the earlier underlying problem, whereas the reality is that X is merely associated with relieving the latter-day present problem. At this stage, the satisfaction feeling gives the illusion of

> fulfilment

A tangle that will have to be unpicked before recovery can begin.

Given that the brain has already registered Stages 1 and 2, the Stage 3 process results in a chemical change in the brain that is experienced as a *need* or *craving*. To Alex it seems like a simple physical equation:

$$do\ X = experience\ satisfaction$$
$$want\ satisfaction = do\ X$$

In fact, what has happened is that the brain has coded the seeming 'satisfaction' of Alex's apparent 'craving' and set up a complex pattern of association which has become a virtual memory of

Stage 1 'I remember feeling bad and that left a wound'
plus Stage 2 'I remember doing X and feeling better'
plus Stage 3 'I remember feeling the desire, doing X, feeling better, and getting satisfaction.'

The virtual memory is experienced by Alex's brain as if it were real and is signalled to the body as a physical craving.

Stage 4 Subsequently

Another brain event in Alex triggers a

bad feeling

which now fires as

need more X

Doing X has now become an activity with pre-programmed connections to the feeling of 'need'. Alex does X, not because it works, as it did in Stage 2, and not because it became a habit, as it did in Stage 3, but because of a belief, given the virtual memory loop, that it *ought* to work as did in Stages 2 and 3, when it was a successful strategy.

At this time, Alex may be building his life around X and nurturing X with other activities. There may even be no obvious reward from X as there was in Stages 2 and 3. Choice is absent and X is taking over.

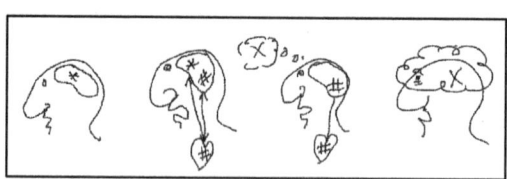

brain event   bad feeling   need more X   X taking over

Stage 4 Subsequently

This four-stage pattern of bodymind events (once upon a time, another time, the next time, subsequently) is encoded in the addictive brain in such a way that each similar subsequent experience only serves to reinforce the supposed 'need'. A memory trace that once related solely to the desire for a present positive experience as a reward for past negative experience has become a 'craving' for X. Each revival of the memory (actually a reconstruction, never the original) is triggered by cues in the present, which may be anything associated with X in the past.

Thus real sensations are reconstructed as virtual obsessions. The desire for X is a mental cue triggering a physical response which has a mental effect.

$$\text{cue} \rightarrow \text{response} \rightarrow \text{effect}$$

A loop that generates an unconscious habit essentially no different to that of a concert pianist playing a complex arpeggio or an artillery gunner performing an intricate drill prompted by the word of command.

When the clock strikes four, I feel the need for a cup of tea and a custard cream. Seeing someone take out a cigarette may prompt another smoker to do the same. Entering a cinema can trigger a sequence of events in the brain which may be experienced as a desire for popcorn. The body experiences the sequence as a craving. And what may have once been a feeling of isolation or sensory deprivation becomes re-interpreted as a need to smoke, drink, have sex, eat chocolate.

These internal and environmental triggers do not have to be obvious or apparent. A withdrawal symptom from addiction can itself become the bad feeling of Stages 2, 3, or 4, triggering a craving and setting off a complex recursive sequence that will be difficult to unravel.

Stage 5 Eventually

The ready-made circuits connect almost simultaneously, triggering a sequence that goes:

$$\text{brain event} \rightarrow \text{bad feeling} \rightarrow \text{can't do without X}$$

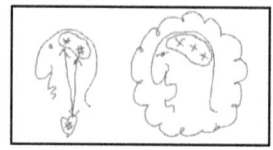

almost simultaneous   X in possession

Stage 5 Eventually

Now X is in possession. It may be very difficult indeed for the sufferer to separate out the components of this sequence without professional help. Alex's experience is of one event. It will be very tempting for him to assume that somehow X is controlling him, rather than that the simultaneity of events is being experienced by him as a lack of control. It is at this stage that the spirit begins to diminish. Thereafter illusion itself will run the loop.

Stage 6 Finally

There may be no respite from emotional overload, leading to mental, spiritual, and physical breakdown.

The mind gives up trying to make sense. Rage and paranoia may overwhelm the personality. Self-harm, suicide, or overdose may result. It is a desperate irony that the addictive process that enabled the personality to survive its early experience of non-being ends in the decline and disintegration of body and mind that the addiction was designed to prevent.

Applying the Model

Facilitators could use this six-stage continuum

> 1 To affirm for themselves and their clients that addictive states of mind do not come from nowhere, but are something we construct from subjective experience.
>
> 2 To track where clients are in their present relationship to X.
>
> 3 To track back with them to likely points for intervention.

4 As a frame of reference when establishing and monitoring therapeutic outcomes. I shall have more to say about therapist and client outcomes in Parts III and IV.

5 Therapists working in Clean Language and Therapeutic Metaphor might like to map across to this structural model from the client's symbolic model on occasion. Sometimes while facilitating a client's metaphoric journey, I feel as if I am tracking a spaceship from a parallel universe and it is nice to get a sense now and again of where everything is in relation to earth.

Conclusion

Physical, or neurophysiological, phenomena (the collection, connection, and interaction of neurons, synapses, receptors, and neurotransmitters in the brain) give rise to mental phenomena (thoughts, feelings, beliefs, consciousness, sense of identity, spirituality, and the like) in the same way that heat is a higher-level emergent property of the motion of molecules of air. Although addictions have a physiological component and may be felt by the addict as physical, the experience of craving is a mental one.

I do not wish to dismiss the feeling of physical addiction, only to expand the way we define it and to question the addictive belief that addiction is a physical process that can only be treated by physical, i.e., medical, means.

It is the physical fact of the evolution of the brain that has produced our higher-order consciousness and ability to think. And our ability to process a thought such as 'physical addiction is actually a mental construction' may help evolve addictive thinking beyond what we once believed to be its physiological limits.

Although each stage of this model of addiction is at a higher level of mental complexity than the one before, each stage can be accessed neurolinguistically. Ways we might do that are many and varied.

▶

Part III
The Physician's Provider

Intemperance is the physician's provider.
Publilius Syrus, Moral Sayings

How do we position ourselves as facilitators in relation to our addictive clients? How can we differentiate between our conscious and unconscious desires? How may we align ourselves with the client's outcome rather than with our outcome for the client?

The deconstruction of addictive thinking supposes the possibility of reconstruction. We know now that our brains are living, changing, adaptable entities. Brain cells make and remake their connections continually; they can alter the strength of their connections over both the short term and the long term; they can develop and retain new connections. Given that billions of brain cells are doing this at every moment and on many levels, it is not fanciful to suggest that the landscape of the addictive mind may be accessed and reconfigured in almost any way the client desires. We can adapt and change.

I am tempted to say we can do this through thought alone, but that requires some explanation. What I mean is we can change through the exercise of our emotional intelligence, which requires the integration of thinking with feeling. Feeling, neuroscientists agree, comes first (it is the anonymous author of most, if not all, the choices and judgements we make) and thinking comes after.[1] 'Emocognition', or the combination of the two, is the emergent outcome of the brain's utilization of sensory experience, intuitive symbol, verbal and nonverbal language, and inner dialogue. Any therapy I can think of makes use of some of these capacities of the human mind, but none in my experience as fully or as mindfully as Clean Language.

The Therapist Prepares

A facilitator working in Clean Language and Therapeutic Metaphor utilizes the client's emocognitive capacity for feeling, symbol, and language at many levels. The exquisite ritual of Clean questioning prompts an inner dialogue with the client's unconscious mental processes, allowing access to self-generated symbolic representations of neural patterns at the boundary between the conscious and unconscious mind. And what happens in response to a well-timed, well-constructed Clean question is that new information pops into consciousness. The client is often surprised by, but rarely rejects, this information, because at some level it is recognized – literally, through re–cognition, or knowing again. The creator of Clean Language, David Grove, called the new-old information tacit knowledge, or "knowledge you don't know you know until you know it."

As re-cognition feeds back into the client's system, a process of multi-level reprocessing takes place in which new neural patterns of association are formed. It is in these neural patterns that the neurochemical change necessary for therapeutic change takes place.

How do facilitators best support this process? Not, I suggest, by trying to 'help'. Helping is co-dependent behaviour.

Addiction to Helping

All the world's ills can be reduced to four things: incomplete communications; thwarted intentions; unfulfilled expectations; and people who try to help.
Laurena Chamlee-Cole after Pat Grove

A client seeking change has to do what a client has to do, not what a therapist, however erudite or empathic, thinks they should do. Growth for the client is about dropping any attachment to the opinions and expectations of others, just as for the therapist it is about dropping any attachment to a personal version of the client's recovery. Co-dependencies thrive on custom and practice. Withdrawal from a relationship with a deferential client may be very difficult indeed for a therapist addicted to the status of one who knows best.

And that is because helping itself can be addictive behaviour. The desperate desire to rescue a client from their victim mind-set; the longing to be indispensable to another human being; the irresistible wish to point travellers in the direction we believe they should travel … all the while imagining ourselves free of any taint of the condition for which we prescribe treatment. Helping can be an addiction little different to alcohol or nicotine dependency: a means of separating the individual – in this case, the client – from their personal resources.

The helper/helped co-dependency is a deep-rooted relationship for helpers brought up, as many were, in families where it was difficult to distinguish between love and control. It has been said more than once that health professionals tend to migrate to professions where they can exercise the supremacy skills they learnt at home.

Here is an instant co-dependency check I have found useful on occasion. Am I advising the client? Reassuring them? Assuming I know what they mean? Believing I know how they feel? If the client is in difficulty, am I trying harder? Am I doing more than half the work in this session? More than, say, ten per cent?

A recovering psychotherapist will aim to separate their unresolved needs from the client's by having an outcome that acknowledges the client as the tutor, not the pupil, in the therapeutic partnership. Clean Language facilitates this postmodern alliance by modelling the person, not the addiction. Addiction, as we have seen, is a concept. I'm not sure how you help concepts change. Indeed, the concepts I know have no desire to change and I wouldn't know how to help one if it did.

Modelling the person rather than the addiction encourages the client to seek personal resources that only they know – often unconsciously – where to locate and how to apply. The change that emerges will be self-authentic and healing self-generated.

Therapist Prejudice

The traditional alternative – modelling the addiction rather than the person – can lead to classifying patient as 'inveterate gamblers' or 'chronic alcoholics' in the same way we bandy about terms like obsessive or manic-depressive. They identify a class, not an individual. Mental patients call it punishment by diagnosis. A whole outside world can be contained in a word. Lumbering a client with a massive container like paranoid or phobic can make the therapist party to a self-fulfilling prophecy. Labels stick.[2]

Once an addictive assumption takes hold in a client at identity level, the therapist can do everything in their power at behavioural and belief levels but get nowhere. One client referred to me by a psychiatrist told me in no uncertain terms, "I have periods of mania and depression, I'm not a manic-depressive." What he sought was escape – not so much from the label as from the presuppositions that came with it. Only then could he begin to treat himself.

Judgment is the inevitable outcome of a prescriptive society in which illness is deemed to be bad for you. It is not the norm in a participative society where illness is explored for the opportunities for growth it affords. Treating addictions and dependencies with drugs alone can mask some of the symptoms and reinforce the systemic structure of addiction by generating further dependency.

>   Bad feeling → Take drug X →
>   Relieve bad feeling → Take more X →
>   Problem with X → Take substitute drug Y →
>   Relieve effects of X → Take more Y →
>   Whether Y works or not → Take more Y →

Drug therapy is as crude a methodology in its way (trial and error) as is much psychotherapy (guesswork). Both can have side effects. Both can be addictive. Yet many psychiatrists would be delighted not to give out drugs if they had enough evidence that psychotherapy 'worked' for addiction. Unfortunately, the belief systems of medical research models are unlikely to produce objective evidence about the subjective experience of one-to-one therapy, while the tenets and limits of one-to-one therapy do not lend themselves convincingly to large-scale randomized trials. We are addicted to our own convictions in these matters.

There is evidence of a little more receptivity between medical and psychological therapies, however. Therapists supporting drug withdrawal in a patient do well to work closely with G.P.s, psychiatrists, staff at specialist clinics, and specialist support groups. Alcohol, heroin, and minor tranquiliser addicts receiving drug treatment for withdrawal may still experience craving and relapse if the underlying psychological components of the addiction are not taken care of. And although I have heard a psychiatrist describe the average withdrawal from substance addiction as "about as bad as a bout of flu," drug therapy may well be indicated alongside psychological therapy if the addict is severely damaged or has life-threatening symptoms. A bad bout of flu, it should be said, can take the sufferer to death's door for days on end.

Not classifying clients is quite different to clients classifying themselves. Until I was able to name my own addictions, I couldn't even begin to think of myself as in recovery. And if you are a therapist or facilitator who believes you have never been dependent on anything, do return to the exercise in understanding on page 12. You will trust yourself more when you have done yourself over. But be warned: knowing yourself better might mean having to give up any notion of knowing what is best for your clients.

Therapist Ethics

Marie is a therapist colleague who worked with one of her clients for the best part of a year before discovering that the client had an alcohol problem. Marie was devastated. Not only had it taken a year for this information to come out, but Marie herself had a distressing family history of alcoholism. An alarm bell rang. Marie had a conditioned reflex. She immediately decided to get her client into Alcoholics Anonymous, because that is what had helped in her own family. Marie made an involuntary systemic connection to an unresolved personal issue. The sequence of internal events probably went something like:

> Hears the word 'alcohol' → Triggers neural pattern of association with 'out of control' → Connects to 'family violence/abuse' neural network → Prompts 'A.A.' memory circuit → Urges client to go to A.A.[3]

I am not saying that Marie was right or wrong in what she did. I am saying that the conditions for addiction and its attendant fears and anxieties are present in us all, and can evoke any number of transference issues that other client conditions may not.[4]

Clean Language has built-in safeguards against transference and so-called counter-transference, but if you work in a traditional model of counselling, your first ethical safeguard might be to align your defining as nearly as you can with your client's. Agree what you mean, for example, by 'quit' and 'control'. If your client simply wants control of their addictive behaviour, but your personal belief about optimal outcomes says that quitting forever is 'better', is it ethically justifiable to continue working with them? It might be if your views are held lightly or if you are able to come clean with your client and remind them of their right of referral. Abstinence is an honourable aim for many, but is not effective for all.

So-called client-centred therapists are expected to reflect on their preconceptions and to share their reactions with the client as part of their 'congruence' in the relationship. Yet an unconditionally client-centred therapist who believed in no interference whatever in client process (I make a distinction between interference – bad – and intervention – neutral) would find it very difficult to say anything at all about themselves without risk of adverse influence on the client's outcome.

It seems to me that a therapist must decide for themself how much or how little of an interventionist they wish to be and to work within those limits. If there were a continuum for therapeutic intervention, I would place Clean questioning at the least interfering end. At the other end I would place 'helping' – offering advice or suggestions based on supposition, interpretation, hypothesis, or ideology – however benign the motive ('it's for your own good,' etc.). The moment we make any assumption that we know what is right for another person, we are on the slippery slope to controlling behaviour. And controlling behaviour is addictive behaviour. It mimics the effects of any drug taken as compensation for unresolved need.

(Un)conscious Outcomes

I would consider my position if I found myself wanting a particular outcome for a client. Want and hope easily shade into expectation, expectation into desire, and desire into will. Even if I had foresworn a conscious outcome, I would almost certainly have formed an unconscious one, and unconscious outcomes are likely to be laden with unwanted baggage. Clean Language has inbuilt checks and balances against such a possibility. It minimizes any temptation I might have to steer the client in a direction I believe to be the only one possible or desirable by my own limited criteria.

My experience over many years with many very different clients leads me to the conviction that at some level, people know what is best for them and that, given the opportunity to generate genuine choice for themselves, will follow a path towards well-being. This may not be the path the therapist would have chosen. If the client's route turns out to be circuitous, the therapist may be reassured that there are likely to be learnings on the way that will be relevant to the client's persona as a whole and not just to the addictive part.

My own outcome is simple: to support clients in making their own choices; to facilitate them towards self-individuation with the least possible contamination (via assumption and suggestion) by me of their process. I do not always achieve this, of course. It is a lot easier if I stick strictly to Clean Language. It is far more difficult if I do not.

A client has to do what a client has to do, after all. Write yourself a note and put it under the pillow.

▶

Notes to Part III

1 *Feeling comes first and thinking after*. For more on the subject, see *How The Brain Feels* (Wayfinder 2012), a guide to working with emotion and cognition.

2 *Paranoid*: a patient seeking a definition of 'paranoia' would find something on the lines of 'mental disorder characterized by delusions of persecution or grandeur, from the Greek for demented.' This describes an extreme condition and is easily misapplied to those who are mistrustful in specific and readily accessible ways. Equally, *phobic* describes someone with an exaggerated fear that is disabling, but is also misapplied to those who are rationally fearful in certain situations and are otherwise well enough.

3 *Alcoholics Anonymous*: many recovering addicts swear by A.A. ('the biggest support system in the world') and some therapists agree to work with alcoholic clients only if they concurrently commit to following an A.A. 12-step programme. However, A.A. encourages clients to swap one dependency (alcohol) for another (the programme), which arguably plays the systemic dependency game. It offers a *translation* of bodymind state in the client rather than a *transformation*. A.A. does not teach clients how to get out of their dependency on the support programme.

NLP addiction counsellor Tina Stacey has designed a '12-state' substance recovery programme as an alternative. The Secular Organization for Sobriety (S.O.S.) has developed a non-religious programme for people with alcohol, eating, and gambling disorders. But there is nothing to compare to A.A.'s ongoing global support system.

4 *Transference and 'counter-transference'*. Whenever any two people come together, there is likely to be some projection of unresolved or inappropriate feelings from one to the other. That is normal. What Clean Language does is minimize its inhibitory, obstructive, or intrusive effects. I don't particularly like the concept of therapist 'counter' transference. It's not 'counter' to client transference and there is nothing special about the way therapists do it. Some psychotherapies incorporate the notion of transference overtly into their work, but this puts their practitioners in a dilemma. If they acknowledge that they may project subjective feelings onto the client derived from the past, it surely undermines their *raison d'être* as objective interpreters of the client's past.

Part IV
Limit of Desires

We would have no reason to find fault with the dissolute if the things that produce its pleasures were able to drive away from their minds their fears about what is above them, and about death and pain, and to teach them the limit of desires. Epicurus, Principle Doctrines

For an unwanted habit to become compulsive, it almost certainly has to take hold at an identity level. "I am a guy who smokes, drinks, does wild stuff," a rock band manager told me, "and my wife wants me to be a guy in a suit." He wanted to give up dope, but not the rest of the wild stuff, because, as he said, "I'm scared who I might turn out to be if I do some heavy change."

Client Issues

If as a sufferer you are uncertain about the extent of your dependency, you might want to ask yourself if you are identifying with your substance or behaviour. "I'm a workaholic." "I'm a woman who has to watch her weight." "I'm a terrible flirt." "I'm a man who likes a flutter." Are you organizing your life around X? Have you ever wondered who you would be without it? Without a secure sense of yourself, well-being may be seen as deriving from what you do or from things external to you.

> Nick defines himself. "I am a smoker," he tells me. He has an image of himself with designer accoutrements (smartphone, branded pack and lighter) and obvious and observable social habits (lighting up with friends on the wine bar terrace). Tokens of belonging. It takes Nick a while to realize that being "a smoker" isn't his authentic self. But he has to honour, not despise, the old Nick before moving on. First, he will get to say, "I am an ex-smoker," and somewhat later, "I am a guy who used to smoke."

It may help to ask yourself what it is you really want. To confront X by quitting? Or to gain some kind of control? Would that be quitting all at once or gradually? Controlling in small steps or big? Or are you just sitting back and assessing, considering whether to do anything at all? Is the desire for change yet present? If so, is the will?

These are important distinctions. And they may change over time as new self-information appears, is recognized, and re-enters your bodymind system. Setting and pursuing an outcome is thus unlikely to be a straightforward linear exercise. Your therapy might need to move forward and back in time without the sequence being obviously sequential. This will be a great deal easier if you and your facilitator approach what you say you want without any preconceptions about what it *should* be. At the start, you might have only the foggiest notion of what you want or, indeed, no notion at all. You can then be questioned on any part of what you come up with in a way that allows you to explore your desired outcome in stages, intuitively and non-cognitively.

Of course, the alternative of committing to an explicit and rational outcome ('I want to cut down to ten a week after the first month and stop altogether by the end of three') may suit you temperamentally, in which case go ahead. There is *no* absolute right answer to the Clean opening question, 'And what would you like to have happen?'

In any model of therapy, your outcome will almost certainly develop, particularly if the addiction is related, as it almost certainly is, to other issues.

> Brian is a bar attendant, who when first asked what he would like to have happen, says, "To sort myself out, there are a few things going on for me." "What kind of things?" I ask. He takes a deep breath. "My girlfriend had an abortion a few months ago, I've had kidney problems for three or four years, I'm depressed, I have a rash on my leg and back, light-headedness, flu, general ill health, I can't deal with people in crowds, I'm drinking too much, my girlfriend gets jealous when I talk to other women, and I've always felt alone."
>
> As you might imagine, it takes a while for Brian to identify one of these as a priority. Eventually he settles on "To give up drinking." Getting this right, he reckons, will help sort out the rest. In the second session, however, his outcome becomes, "To control the depression." And in the third (by which time we are working in Therapeutic Metaphor process), "Clear thinking. A filter for the impurities." He is able to identify that a filter for the impurities will clarify his thinking, which will help lift his depression, which will give him less cause for drinking.

The Clean opening question 'And what would you like to have happen?' can lead to the unfolding of any number of issues. If you are doing X as a substitute for authentic human connection, your X could relate to any aspect of the human condition. You may wonder whether the addiction is a mask for other disorders or whether other disorders are a mask for the addiction. Which came first? There is a pragmatic answer to these chicken-or-egg questions: it depends which disorder you acknowledge first or which you wish to work on first. Finding out more about the chicken will be your royal route to the egg, and vice versa.

Desire – Need – Possession

How do you personally define your state or behaviour? Where would you place yourself on a 'desire → need → possession' continuum? (See Client Presentations, page 37) Do you reckon you can 'take it or leave it'? Can you 'stop any time'? Or do you speak in terms of 'must have' or 'always do'?

At this point, your facilitator really needs to suspend judgement about the meaning of what you say and pay attention to your actual words. Client definitions and desires are highly subjective, and that makes them wide open to misinterpretation. No two people will view or express anything in exactly the same way.

Here are a few statements from my own client notes:

> "I'm strongly attached" (smoking problem)
> "It's a physical craving" (smoking)
> "A need to fill myself like a garbage can" (chocolate)
> "Finding an escape" (alcohol)
> "Blotting out" (alcohol)
> "I'm running round in circles" (idealism)
> "There's like a wall around me" (anger)

These happen to be metaphors.[1] There is key information in the way that the speakers have constructed them, but what is it and how can they get to it? Metaphor is an enormously valuable intermediary between problem and solution in that it mediates the interface between the conscious and unconscious mind. These symbolic expressions of the clients' relationship with their addictions are ripe with the promise of new information through non-assumptive questioning.

And when you're strongly attached, what kind of 'attached' could that attached be?"
It's as if there is a heavy rope with someone on the other end pulling me.

And is there anything else about that someone on the other end pulling you?
Oh, it's my father.

The more information you have about yourself as client, the more you will have a sense of running the show rather than the show running you. The feeling of being possessed by, rather than possessing, an addiction or compulsion arises from the sense that the related behaviour is somehow outside your control; that your internal state is governed by an external thing. A part has power over the whole and your freedom of choice is limited or non-existent.

Sooner than later, it is likely that you will arrive at a point where you need to separate the internal feeling (+ve or –ve) from the external substance or activity, so that one is not in thrall to the other.

$$\text{internal state} / \quad / \text{external X}$$

Separation, mental or physical, is not in itself a resolution of the problem, but is the key to opening the door to resolution in almost every case. What presently connects your state of mind and X? In terms of the Part II model, we might characterize it as an interaction of neuronal groupings in the brain acting on the primary motor cortex that sends impulses to muscles prompting specific behaviour. Or, if you prefer, you feel bad and do X. Which in the early stages of addiction, at least, leads to feeling good.

$$\text{bad feeling} \rightarrow \text{do X} \rightarrow \text{feel good}$$

A good facilitator can help you intervene to effect in this sequence of bodymind connections, but meanwhile if you can

$$\text{name} \rightarrow \text{acknowledge} \rightarrow \text{own} \rightarrow \text{take responsibility for}$$

your addiction (not always as pain-free a chain of behaviours as it may sound), you will be taking a significant first step towards sorting it out. And sorting starts from the moment you and your facilitator begin to gather information together.

Client Presentations

Consider four client statements on the lines of:

> "I can take it or leave it."
> "I can stop any time I want."
> "I'm not hooked, you know."
> "I can't give up, and I must give up."

Which comes nearest to yours at this time? As a facilitator, I would be concerned if you went on to claim marriage or work problems rather than dependency problems. I might be tempted to challenge that or – more cleanly, perhaps – work with the other problem you have identified as a way into the addiction issue. I would also watch out if you had switched from one addiction to another to prove to yourself that you were not addicted to the first. Or if you were to say, "I find myself eating for the same reasons I used to smoke." Or if you were so deeply immured in the secret world of your addiction that you attempted to hide it from me. A rational part of you would be seeking something, but an inaccessible or diseased part would be preventing you from admitting it.

"I can take it or leave it"

So why are you here? What haven't you dealt with? The compulsion to count the spoons every day might be under your control for the moment, but if the underlying issue stays unresolved, the compulsion will return. At what stage of the Part II model would you place yourself? Stage 3, perhaps: 'desire' shading into 'need'. If you and your facilitator were to track back desire to a time when 'bad feeling' became entangled with 'X' to produce apparent 'satisfaction', you would almost certainly get a sense of a place or places to work.

Meanwhile, I am irresistibly drawn to non-assumptive questioning of what you have said. "And when you can take it, what kind of 'it' could that 'it' be?" "And when you can leave it, what kind of 'it' could that 'it' be?" (It may not be the same as the first 'it') "And that is a 'take it or leave it' like what?" Do you have a symbolic sense of your 'take or leave'?

With a nebulous statement like 'I can take it or leave it,' I find myself wondering if something is missing. Perhaps a core sense of self which you have not yet been able to access. "And is there anything else about the 'I' that can take it or leave it?" "And that is an 'I' that can take it or leave it like what?"

An alternative approach would be to explore that part of you which might be objecting to a commitment to dealing with the problem. What is its positive intention and how might that be reframed?[2]

"I can stop any time I want"

Are you using addictive (false) logic to explain things away? Or do you have an intuitive sense of another issue, which the addiction is masking? What kind of change do you want? In what kind of way? My guess is that if you are talking like this, you have already begun to look into yourself. You may be somewhere in Stage 4 – 'need' or 'craving' – and getting concerned. "And is there anything else about the 'I' that 'can stop'?" "And is there a relationship between the 'I' that 'can stop'" and the 'I' that 'wants'?" And so on.

"I`m not hooked, you know"

That may be, but I wonder if you are in denial. A.A. calls alcoholism "cunning, baffling, powerful … and patient." Or perhaps you are right by your own definition, in which case I might ask you what you mean. "And what kind of 'hooked', 'at the mercy of,' etc.?" It's possible that you are in Stage 4, 'need' or 'craving', shading into Stage 5, 'can't do without'.

Alternatively, we could explore the metaphorical sense of your non-addiction.

> And when not hooked, that is not hooked like what?
> *It's like I'm thrashing about in shallow waters.*
>
> And is there anything else about those shallow waters?
> *The water is draining away, it's getting difficult to breathe.*

The 'like what?' question draws attention to the possibility of an unconscious metaphorical function for what I might otherwise have dismissed as an empty everyday cliché.

> I have been working with Dmitri for several weeks. He is clever, sharp, and charming. He has identified what he calls "potential addictions to smoking and overwork," which, he claims, "do not totally possess" him. It sounds like another way of saying, 'I'm not

hooked.' What these "potential addictions"' want for him, he discovers after extended work, is "self-respect". But every time Dmitri gets a glimpse of self-respect, something else intrudes and stops him achieving it. What is this thing and what does it want? Every time Dmitri gets a sense of the person he wants to be, he loses concentration, drifts away, and starts to think about other things; then stress kicks in and he closes down. Sometimes he has to go outside for a smoke. I sense that closing down is a far more powerful compulsion than smoking and overwork, but is just not ready to give up the information it holds.

We shall return to Dmitri a little later.

"I can`t give up and I must give up"

The classic Cartesian (duality thinking) dilemma. You are trapped in the narrow strait controlled by those sea monsters Scylla and Charybdis. Escaping the jaws of one leads only to being devoured by the other. 'Can't give up' has you possessed by Scylla. 'Must give up' has you fearing Charybdis more.[3]

Definitions first: does your 'can't' means 'don't want to' or 'choose not to'? I might ask,

> And what kind of 'can't' could that 'can't give up' be?"

And does your 'must' mean 'should' or 'have to'?

> And what kind of 'must' could that 'must give up' be?

It makes a difference, you will discover, as the questions sink in.

What unstated rules may be operating here? Addicts and their co-dependents often believe that there is only one right way of being in the world. They have absorbed a cultural value that says they should be one thing or the other. Addicted or abstinent. Right-brained or left. Secure or free. Naughty or nice. Anyone who is, or wishes to be, both, or something between, or cannot decide, is beyond the pale.

Excessive internal conflict can be created by these can't/must swings. They may build to a crisis that can be resolved only by following the path of least resistance, which usually means giving in to the addiction … at which point a further paradox rears its head, as addiction evokes the very affect it has been seeking to prevent: isolation, fear and pain. Duality thinking is an addictive illness, and paradox and contradiction are its terrible twin symptoms. How may they be treated?

▶

Notes to Part IV

1 *Client metaphors*: the word 'craving' is not quite a metaphor, but is ambiguous. Its generally accepted meaning is a strong or overwhelming desire, but only a few decades ago it meant an authoritative, if mock-polite, demand: 'I crave leave to observe …' It might be interesting to discover if someone (real or imagined) is demanding something of the client who has a physical 'craving' and if so on what authority or by what right.

2 *NLP reframing*, or what Pamela Gawler-Wright calls, "integrating the hidden purpose of the problem." For full details of the technique, see Bandler and Grinder, *Reframing: NLP and the Transformation of Meaning*, Real People Press 1982. Reframing an addictive 'part' may be difficult if the client manifests what B & G call "sequential incongruity", where the therapist has access to the sober, non-X part of the client, which wants to change, but not to the X part, which almost certainly doesn't. B & G take the reader through an advanced technique for changing 'sequential' into 'simultaneous' by separately anchoring X and non-X states, firing them simultaneously, and obliging them to co-exist. Needs care.

3 *Caught between Scylla and Charybdis*: my personal metaphor for the addictive dilemma. In a facilitative situation, a Clean facilitator would never bring up such an image. The client's metaphor would be the only one that was relevant.

Part V
Resolving Addictive Contradictions

*We shall never understand anything until
we have found some contradiction.*
Niels Bohr

Towards the end of Part IV, we began to deconstruct the typically addictive duality

> I can't give up X and I must give up X

Statements like this are a linguistic lure. The client may be tempted into believing there is some kind of intellectual justification for their irresolution: 'I am trapped in a perfect bind. There is nothing I can do. To escape from the frying pan means only to die in the fire.'

Is our two-handedness a part of the problem? 'On the one hand this, on the other hand that.' Or the mind-body split? 'My head tells me this … my heart … ' In normal circumstances, we know that it is perfectly possible to feel both love and hate, rich and poor, joy and despair together. Contradictory feelings are the twin dynamic that drives our lives. They do not normally incapacitate us. In the parallel world of addiction, however, the experience of being stranded between the poles of aversion and attraction can be bewildering and intolerable. The feeling that it is also irresolvable – that there is no way of finding our bearings in this existential wasteland – can make it spectacularly worse.

Recognizing the contradiction contained in 'I can't give up X and I must give up X' at least allows it to be challenged. The trick is to recognize it.

> Every time Dmitri tries to talk about what he calls his "potential" addictions to smoking and overwork, he "closes down". This closing down part has been doing its job so well over eight two-hour sessions that it has refused to allow him to know anything about itself. Now grudgingly it allows him to give it a name. And its name, unsurprisingly, is "negativity". So secretive and disapproving has negativity been throughout Dmitri's life that whenever he starts to open up and feel good about himself, he finds himself involuntarily closing down. "Blanks" and "blocks" appear in his language, but

> refuse, even under the cleanest of Clean questioning, to divulge their nature.
>
> Dmitri has to be very creative indeed to trick negativity into showing itself long enough to be identified. And gradually the paradox that has held all this in place emerges: negativity has had a positive historical intention for him. It originated in an attempt to protect him from sickening violence and abuse when as a child he was naturally open and vulnerable.

We can see in Dmitri's process how the normal dynamic of aversion and attraction has been reversed. Aversion, instead of being a negative force, which would have helped him survive in normal circumstances (to avoid pain or injury, for example), in this instance became a positive force (aversion from addiction being an attraction towards health). And attraction, instead of being a positive force, as it would have been in normal times of survival (a craving for water to satisfy thirst, say), became negative (attraction to X is a move away from health). Such inversion reflects abnormal conflict.

> Eleanor is a manager in the middle of a painful divorce. Her first statement to me is, "I can't give up my anger and I have to get rid of my anger." She goes on, "I'm running round in circles." I acknowledge her stuckness: "And you're running round in circles." I draw her attention to her stuckness: "And you're running round in circles ... and you're running round in circles ..." And I question her stuckness: "And when you're running round in circles, what happens next?" "I don't know," she replies. "I can't get off."

How may binds like Dmitri's and Eleanor's, which have been in place for many years and are functioning perfectly – as binds – be persuaded to transform into something more amenable to resolution (if that is what they want)? Some clients fear freedom more than the binds that tie them. Others yearn desperately to unpick their tangled patterns.

David Grove would say, "Within the paradigm of the presentation of the problem lies also the solution." The first step is to find out what the client actually wants. What is *their* solution to the problem?

> *And when blanks and blocks appear, what would you like to have happen?*
>
> *And when you're running round in circles and can't get off, what would you like to have happen?*

Dmitri may be moved to confront or avoid his blocks and blanks. Eleanor may wish to stop going round, or to go round another way or for a while longer.

The resolution of a stuck state is not to be sought in the dualism from which it often derives. Dualism would have us believe that categories of stopping or continuing, confrontation or avoidance, can't or must, are mutually exclusive endpoints. We can shuffle back and forth between them on occasion, but that only gives us the illusion of control without the reality of the power necessary to resolve them. To give ourselves more room for manoeuvre, we need to open up these restrictive, addictive, mind-languaging limitations we impose on ourselves.

Here are a number of approaches to examining addictive contradictions, discovering what impels them, and freeing ourselves from their endless embrace. They are admitting third options, negotiating, escaping, counter double-binding, changing the rules, metaphor modelling, converging, and allowing.

Admitting Third Options

The universe of which we are a negligible part is more subtle, multiple, and sensible than our earthbound 'either-or' limits allow. In the quantum domain, for example, it is generally accepted nowadays that light behaves not just as a 'wave' or a 'particle', but somehow as both. Our intellects and imaginations have some catching up to do.

Freeing ourselves from dualistic (dyadic) thinking means moving to third options. Not, note, to a single third option, when it becomes no more than triadic thinking. Mao Tse-Tung optimistically declared the dialectical contradiction of things, 'the law of the unity of opposites' – a revolutionary reframe that turned the dyadic thinking of the day (a belief in irreconcilable opposites) on its head, yet produced only one alternative (supposed 'unity') and what is more, made it an absolute ('the law'). This turned out to be a pretty limited third option.

Examples of limiting, self-reinforcing triadic thinking in therapy are the three-legged victim-persecutor-rescuer co-dependency, the child-parent-adult psychodrama triangle, and NLP's self-other-observer perceptual positions.

	victim		child		self	
persecutor		rescuer	parent	adult	other	observer

They can be useful staging posts on the road from duality thinking to more open possibilities, but they are not destinations in themselves. Victim-persecutor-rescuer need more choices; child-parent-adult need more relations; self-other-observer benefit from further community, universal, and spiritual (to name but a few) systemic perceptual positions.[1]

Philosopher-mathematician Bart Kosko, author of Fuzzy Thinking, summed up the solution as "Paradox at endpoints, resolution at midpoints." He did not say 'at midpoint'.

> Colin is a client, a City trader addicted to cocaine. He discovers that in his problem pattern (too many decisions to make, too little time in which to make them) lies also his salvation (neither to go mad nor to opt out – the duality non-choice – but to allow and enjoy life's drug-free infinite variety). He recognizes that he has *an infinite number of third options*. Moving to any one of them transcends the apparent logic of his conflict.

Negotiating

Conflicting endpoints can be encouraged to negotiate. NLP has a powerful technique for moderating the conspicuously incompatible elements of a bind ('on the one hand this, on the other hand that'). The client is encouraged to fully express the two contradictory elements of the bind, to achieve clear contact between them, and from a meta-position have them interact. The polarities can be coached to combine into a third thing or to negotiate how best to utilize each other's skills. The premise behind the technique is that every polarity is an actual or potential resource, and that a combination of resources offers the client significantly more advantage than can be derived from a solitary resource.

Another kind of negotiation aimed at resolving internal conflict came from the work of U.S. therapist Virginia Satir in the 1970s and 80s. One member of a therapeutic group is invited to identify and name a number of conflicting parts of themselves (Jolly Roger, The Critic, Speedy Gonzales, and so on), to cast them as characters from other members of the group, and to coach them in how they would behave in a social interaction. The parts are then invited to a party and their owner observes the chaos that typically ensues. The party is stopped, the owner coaches a couple of the more disruptive characters in how to behave differently, and the party continues. It is not always a roaring success, but is usually less chaotic.

Escaping

If you are ever caught in a quicksand, you may feel helpless, believing that either doing nothing or struggling violently will only drag you down further. This is generally true, but there is a midpoint solution. If you wiggle your legs slowly, you will gradually create a space through which water will flow to loosen the density of the sand, which will help you float so that you may more easily escape.

> Daniel is an IT consultant whose marriage has failed. He has an obsession with being right, which not surprisingly he has found to be incompatible with the compromise necessary for sharing his life with someone. In his first session of therapy, Daniel traces his problem back to adolescence and the feeling of intellectual superiority he had over friends whose games he wanted to join in with. The *desire* to express his brilliance and yet not express it led to his *possession* by the apparently insoluble duality of the situation. He is riven by the need for both intellectual separation and social inclusion.
>
> In his third session, Daniel spontaneously identifies a solution to the bind – instead of *both* dividing and combining himself (irreconcilable extremes), he realizes that he can do *either at different times* (allowing choice), a neat little wiggle that transcends the apparent logic of the bind. It gives him space to escape the old pattern and to view it from a new perspective.

Here are three typical binds that can be outwitted, sidestepped, circumvented, or otherwise wiggled out of:

1 *I can't decide between A and B.*
2 *I can't decide between A and B because I'm stupid.*
3 *If I continue smoking I'll die young, but if I stop smoking I'll go mad.*

In the first, a simple A–B dilemma is held in place by the client's inability to decide. In the second, the client has added a further layer of inhibition. The lower level double-bind ('I can't decide between A and B) is held in place by a higher level third ('I'm stupid'). In the third example, the perceived bind of dying young by continuing to smoke is held in place by the perceived bind of going mad by stopping.

The demands of a double-bind are by definition irreconcilable. The client can struggle forever attempting to reconcile two mutually exclusive aspirations or to decide between two equally unacceptable options.

Yet the first bind – 'I can't decide between A and B' – can be outwitted in several ways: by making a decision one way or the other; by committing to go with whichever option comes up on the toss of a coin; by first resolving the inability to decide; or by reframing the choice – for example, by allowing that 'Both A and B have advantages, which advantage do I prefer?' or conversely, 'Both A and B have disadvantages, which disadvantage do I find less undesirable?'

The second bind – 'I can't decide between A and B because I'm stupid' – requires more wiggle space. Redefining the limiting belief to 'I'm not stupid, I can solve this,' will lead to a decisive weakening of the inhibition on making a decision that is holding the A–B bind in place. This will free the client to face the dilemma, which will no longer be so formidable.

In the third – 'If I continue smoking I'll die young, but if I stop smoking I'll go mad' – the therapist may challenge the supposed logic of the complex equivalence by asking, 'How does stopping smoking mean going mad?,' or may open up the frame by putting the less challenging question, 'And what is the relationship between stopping smoking and going mad?' Either option will work to clear the information pathway and make more space in which to seek a solution. An alternative would be to reduce the over-elaborate edifice the client has constructed to its essential can't/must framework – 'I can't give up smoking and I must give up smoking' – and proceed to work on it as a normal duality.

If any of the limiting beliefs that hold these binds in place ('I can't decide,' 'I'm stupid,' 'I'll die young,' 'I'll go mad') are strongly enough held, they will resist all attempts to outwit them. Equally, if a limiting belief is out of the client's awareness – an unconscious fear that giving up X will precipitate something worse, say – it may be difficult to tease out. Psychotherapist Penny Tompkins quotes the case of an unhappily married alcoholic who could not give up drinking because of an unconscious belief that if he got better and was true to himself, he would have to leave his wife and separate from his children. A confusing, but not impossible, conundrum. The client and his family needed time and space to work this one out.

Counter Double-Binding

It has been said that the nearer we are to paradox, the nearer we are to healing. Counter (therapeutic) double-binding, or 'paradoxicalizing', is an art form that depends on the creative intuition of the moment in the context of the therapeutic relationship as a whole. 'As you stop drinking, would you like to do it now or over the next two weeks?' is a relatively simple example. And to fully appreciate hypnotherapist Milton Erickson's classic attempt at directing a client to become autonomous with the injunction, "Disobey me!", we have to imagine the extent of his rapport with the client and the history of the client's lifetime struggle with self-assertion.

Counter double-binding is about confounding client logic by working within the client's own rules. It is a subject all of its own (read Bateson, Rossi, Haley, Palazzoli, Laing et al), so I shall confine myself to one aspect here. To have the fullest possible chance of inducing change, a counter double-bind should contain an incentive to the client to rise above the divide represented by the A–B duality. Putting the client into a further bind can – paradoxically – provide that incentive.

A paradox is something seemingly self-contradictory or absurd, yet possibly well founded or true. Note that 'seemingly', 'or', 'yet,' and 'possibly': the paradoxical intent is to confuse the left brain so that the right rewrites the rules – which can only be read by the left! If your mind is boggled by that, you will have some idea how a client in paradox feels. Self-healing is not going to happen without supreme effort and a radical shift.

Here is an example, a paradoxical intervention designed by therapist Pamela Gawler-Wright after work by Ian McDermott. It involves eliciting from the client all the advantages to be gained from their addictive behaviour, followed by listing all the positive values those advantages represent. When the list is complete, the therapist conscientiously reiterates every personal value that the client has identified – taste, fun, sociability, self-affirmation, etc. – and asks two further questions:

"And X gives you all these things?"
"Yes," says the client.
"And would you like more of all these?"
"Yes!" says the client (they are pretty unlikely to say no).
"Then all you have to do is more X!" exclaims the therapist.

For a moment, the client's psychic integrity is threatened. The therapist has sprung a therapeutic trap, designed to create confusion and an internal dissembling of the duality. The bodymind system needs to make sense of this unexpected absurdity before it can be at ease again.

'Uh? If I do more X, I benefit. How's that work? I thought I said I wanted to stop X. So if I refuse to do X, I benefit. Or do I? How? How can I get the benefits of that list of good things I get from X without doing X?'

A question only the client can answer.

Changing the Rules

If the current rules, which include personal beliefs and cultural injunctions, do not produce a solution, they need to be amended or transcended. The riddle of the Gordian knot is said to have inspired a certain creativity in Alexander the Great. It had been prophesied that whoever should loosen this ingenious knot would be the ruler of all Asia. Many tried to unravel the knot before Alexander came along, took out his sword, and cut the knot in two. He included and transcended a generally accepted rule about how knots should be 'loosened'.

Every way of resolving an addictive contradiction involves a change to the rules of the game. Addictive thinking has an all-inclusive rule that says, 'A *excludes* B'. Admitting third options changes the corollary that says, 'there is *only* A and B' to 'there is a lot more than A and B.'

Transcending the logic of a bind changes a rule that says, 'binds require logic to resolve them' into 'logic is not all they need.'

Mao's 'unity of opposites' rewrote a rule of philosophy that said 'opposites are disunified'.

My client Daniel's "I can be both smart and nice" rewrote a rule he imbibed as a child that said he had to be one or the other.

Negotiating changes a belief that goes, 'either A or B must win' into 'A and B can work together so that neither will lose.'

Paradoxicalizing challenges the convention that therapists help their clients and replaces it with 'you have to sort this out for yourself.' It arouses the bodymind tendency to equilibrium through a critical change to its comfort level. The system must resolve the reversal before it can experience comfort and stability again.

Metaphor Modelling

Clean questioning of client metaphor changes a rule that says 'people change behaviourally or miraculously or after many years of analysis.' The client is facilitated to develop and transform the bind at the point where the deliberate and the intuitive parts of the mind connect and interact – in metaphor. Reorganizing the perplexing elements of a limiting bind into the unlimited potential of a metaphor landscape is a way of honouring complexity without sacrificing clarity.

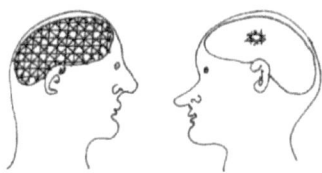

Honouring complexity without sacrificing clarity

For many clients, the development of a metaphor landscape in the form of a mental map, a two-dimensional drawing, or a three-dimensional *mise en scène* becomes a context for the metamorphosis of binds which cannot be resolved within their own apparent 'logic'.[2] A metaphor can carry a substantial amount of information, including experience of trauma, aggregated into a safer, more accessible, more transmutable form.

> Daniel is the IT consultant ('Escaping', page 45) who was unable to enjoy his own talents. He had worked out that the insoluble bind of wishing to both divide and combine himself (to separate from his peers intellectually while associating with them socially) had a simple solution: he could do either at different times. Now something else is troubling him. He admits to being addicted to overwork. "I can't stop working and I must stop working," he says. In Therapeutic Metaphor process, he identifies a "twist" in his

stomach as the source of his pain. I (privately) suppose this to be a variation on the knot, a classic container for historical trauma. "And what kind of twist could that twist be?" I ask. "It's like a tightly twisted cord," is his reply. Daniel works on this pattern for the rest of the session. His homework is to research the word 'twist'.

At the next session, Daniel reports on a Middle English derivation he has discovered – not of the noun, but of the verb. 'To twist' originally meant an improbable combination of *both* 'divide into two' and 'combine into one.' "How is that possible?" he asks. He has created another insoluble bind. I invite him to draw out his twisted cord on the flip chart. As he does so, he recalls the miserable time he had at school and the extreme difficulty he had as a seven-year old holding himself back academically so that he did not have to go to classes two years ahead of his friends. To combine with his friends, he divided himself – separating the gifted one who was intellectually superior from the social one who wanted to play.

Daniel's rule as a child had been 'you cannot have the best of both worlds.' Over the years, he has developed this into a rule that says, 'doing contradictory things is impossible.'

I invite him to continue 'drawing out' the twisted cord. He does so, literally and metaphorically. The cord is made up of several strands and each strand has a certain quality. Daniel relates these to his own qualities. The impossibility of enjoying them separately or together is no longer the rule. He is beginning to transcend the logic of his presentation of the problem.

Converging

This beguiling method of exploring addictive duality was created by NLP researcher Sid Jacobson. Each part of the duality is tracked separately back in time until *a common imprint* appears. It is this point of convergence at which we work.

A client with a 'must X' / 'must not X' duality is asked a series of 'What *led to* 'must X'?' questions followed by a series of 'What *led to* 'must not X'?' questions.

> What led Nick, a journalist client, to "Must smoke" was "Smoking". Asked what led him to smoking, he identifies "Wanting to smoke." Tracking back further takes him to "A combination of taste and opportunity." Further back still, he arrives at "Kissing a girl in a cowshed in Cumbria."

> Quite separately, Nick tracks the other strand of his duality. What led him to "Must not smoke" was "Wanting to feel healthier." Before that, "Breathing freely", which came from "Walking and climbing", which was prompted (you guessed) by "Kissing a girl in a cowshed in Cumbria."

Nick's first adolescent experience of sex had become entangled in his mind with both positive and negative anchors for smoking. The Part II neurobiological model gives us an idea of how this can happen.

Make of this exercise in convergence what you will (and it points to the highly idiosyncratic nature of common imprints and the near-impossibility of predicting them), but in less than an hour Nick had information about his addiction that might otherwise have been hidden forever. Probably in the cowshed.

The principle of convergence changes a rule that says, 'different things come from different places' into 'apparently different things can come from the same place.'

Allowing

Simply allowing a contradiction changes an injunction many of us have that says, 'Everything worthwhile is the result of struggle.' When it comes to two impossibly contradictory things, perhaps the simplest way of dealing with them – and paradoxically for some, hardest of all – is just to allow them.

Daniel has already shifted his perception of the bind he is in from the insoluble (I cannot enjoy my special talents because it separates me from others) to the feasible (I can express myself differently as I choose). The choice he has now may be more a translation of his state of mind than a transformation. He is still playing the game by its own rule of two, believing he has to be one thing or the other.

> At the end of session twelve, Daniel makes what seems to be a qualitatively different shift. It sounds obvious when he says it – I wonder why he hasn't he thought of doing this before – but in the context of the emotionally charged patterns of Daniel's life, I recognize its potential for transforming his whole way of being in the world. "I can be happier if I just allow the combining and dividing," he says. "Being a part of ordinary society while enjoying

my own special talents. I will be happier as I allow them. Yes. This sits well."

I see him embody the learning as he speaks. He just looks physically more comfortable. "Is there anything else about that allow?" I ask. "Well, allowing them to both combine and divide is not the same as giving in to either. And I'm not fighting them. I'm just, you know, allowing them." I believe from his smile that he is probably transcending them.

Daniel has made a useful distinction – part intuitive, part reactive – between allowing and giving in. He goes on to call this third thing "accepting". He is happy enough with the new pattern of healing he has created, but a couple of sessions later, goes further still. He decides that "accepting" is just one option: the third corner of a 'fighting – giving in – accepting' triangle. If you remember Kosko's "paradox at endpoints, resolution at midpoints," Daniel is at a midpoint. Towards the end of the session, he says, "Actually, there are a hundred ways of accepting between the extremes of fighting and giving in. And that is easier to do than creating exactly the right third option."

▶

Notes to Part V

1 *NLP perceptual positions process*: see O'Connor and Seymour, *Introducing NLP*, The Aquarian Press 1990 and Q19 of Part VI.

2 *Clean questioning of a spatially organized bind:* a detailed case history of the resolution of a bind using Therapeutic Metaphor and Emergent Knowledge process is to be found in Chapter 5, Part V, of my book, *The Power of Six*. The client was a life coach who had a small apartment in Paris and needed money for a bigger space. She believed that the way to get more money was to have more corporate clients, but she couldn't get more corporate clients until she had money for a bigger space. A nice double-bind, which she went on to resolve.

Part VI
Auditing for X

Audit: a hearing of accounts
Auditor: one who learns by aural instruction

Whatever the difficulties, being witness as facilitator/auditor to the emergence of client self-reliance is as fulfilling and considerable an experience as bringing new life into the world. If intemperance is the physician's provider, the provision will not only be difficulty, but also delight.

Stefan is a 31-year old entrepreneur who has come into therapy saying he feels helpless, he has never been able to concentrate, his marriage has fallen apart, and he hates himself. As he speaks, he is constantly distracted. He has to break off to go outside for a cigarette. When he returns, I ask him what he wants. He doesn't know. It might be to stop smoking. I try to elicit a metaphor for what he initially described as his helplessness, but he appears not to understand my questions. So I begin to ask him a series of very basic questions about the manifestly obvious – where, when, what, and how does he smoke?

As we plod painstakingly through the most elementary of audits of Stefan's twenty-a-day habit, he begins to reveal more of himself *to himself*. Soon he is confessing to something he has managed to disown for seventeen years. Since the age of fourteen, Stefan has wanted revenge on an uncle who cheated his father out of the family business. Stefan has been consumed by this desire for revenge and yet for all these years he has been denying it, diverting it, and depriving it of any dignity it may have had.

After several sessions, Stefan discovers what underlies both his nicotine dependency and his desire for revenge. His voice drops. He has difficulty describing it. "It's anger", he says. "It's shameful, it's shocking. It's just not me. I've never lifted a finger against anyone." At the end of an uncomfortable session, he is able to say, "I've never acknowledged my anger before, it's never been heard. It's not necessarily bad in itself. I'm not really a bad person." His face is softer and for the first time since we began working together, the words aren't tumbling out of him like scared rabbits.

Unaddicting is unlikely to be easy. Its course is often elusive and difficult to track. An addiction may be obscured by unrelated behaviours or may underlie other dependencies. How has the client constructed their personal mix? How can a facilitator help activate change without resorting to subjective supposition, uncertain interpretation, and superfluous suggestion?

In Stefan's case, my audit helped him identify smoking as an idiosyncratic distraction to a feeling of severe helplessness. The helplessness resulted from the lack of resolution of a long-standing, barely expressed desire for revenge. The desire for revenge concealed a further layer of frustration arising from his unwillingness to accept a deeply disturbing feeling of anger. Every case is different. Stefan went on to reveal a history of childhood abuse, which had a direct structural relationship to his anger, helplessness, frustration, and smoking. A client who has never sifted through the history of X may uncover many layers.

The questionnaire that follows is designed to help addictive, compulsive, or dependent clients account for, get to know, and to trust their own (internal) process. It is a participatory audit that takes the client into four frames I call

> Person: how much of the client is involved and where?
>
> Possession: what is the nature of the client's attachment and how strong is it?
>
> Pattern: how do the client's life patterns and internal structural patterns relate?
>
> Preference: what choices does the client have?

Self-knowledge itself becomes the catalyst of change. As new information, or the re-cognition of existing information, re-enters the self-system, the system will re-organize. As James Lawley has said:

> *Self-reflective questioning can effectively assist someone to completely reorganize their cognitive/conceptual structure, with the ripple effect influencing 'deeper' organizing metaphors, embodied experience and neuro-chemical processes.*

The four frames of the questionnaire are in generally ascending order, with what should be the least challenging frame first. Questions that acknowledge a negatively connoted past are set in the accessible present ('What is …?' 'What are …?') on the premise that the present moment is the only one that really exists. Questions that anticipate a positive future are again phrased in the present ('What is …?' 'What may …?'), on the premise that a non-dependent state of abstinence or control is available now. The addictive past is not assumed to constitute an immutable future, but to contain presently available resources.

The underlying presupposition of the audit is the need for the client to separate their internal state (+ve or –ve) from their external X, so that one is not in thrall to the other; 'X' being the addiction, compulsion, or dependency, or the condition from which the addiction has emerged.

A note for self-helpers: it is not necessary to have a qualified therapist take you through this questionnaire, though if difficult issues arise, you may wish to have professional support to relieve you of the responsibility of holding them alone. Be aware that the further you get into this questionnaire, the more such support you may need.

It may not be necessary to plough through every question in each frame. The moment for a specialist intervention – moving into Therapeutic Metaphor, Clean Space, or Power of Six process, for example – may occur at any time. But each question is a reflective intervention in its own right. The distinctive reappearance of patterns in response to different questions will have its own re-educative effect.

As you work through this audit, I recommend that you welcome repetition, embrace the obvious, and bear in mind that any one question may prove to be the key to a significant shift in the client's self-understanding, acceptance, and readiness to change.

Information Activating and Change Questionnaire

As soon as you start asking questions, you start loosening stuckness.
Alistair Rhind

Person

How much of the client has been involved in the addiction? Thirteen questions based on levels of subjective experience: primary (self interacting with environment; secondary (beliefs about self); tertiary (beliefs beyond self).

1 Primary level (self interacting with environment)

Q1 *What has been the general context of X for you? And specifically?*

X has not existed in isolation. In what surroundings and with whom did X manifest itself? Home, work, school, alone, social situations, significant relationships, casual relationships?

Q2 *Are there influences outside yourself?*

In the environment, society, family, peer pressure, cultural expectation, advertising, availability or non-availability of resources (wealth, indulgence, poverty, deprivation, etc.)?

Q3 *What help is available or possible for you in Q1 and Q2 contexts?*

Q4 *What specifically may you change in Q1 and Q2 contexts so that they are more helpful?*

Q5 *What specifically have you done in relation to X?*

And specifically how? Discounting for the moment any interconnection with other levels of experience, what does the client actually do that causes the problem? What is the relevant behaviour?

Q6 *What may you actually do or do differently for change?*

Requires the client to identify the specific 'cue' event or behaviour. What happens just before doing X? And what happens just before that? It may be possible to work on this moment to generate a compelling alternative behaviour to the learned/conditioned response.

Q7 *Which of your skills/capabilities/resources/strategies enables X?*

The assumption is that application and energy have been required. In rehearsing this question, the client will be primed for answering the next.

Q8 *Which of your skills/capabilities/resources/strategies will enable X to change?*

An appeal to client creativity. How can Q7 answers crossover into Q8 territory? What further skills etc. may be helpful? There may be benefit for the client in learning relaxation, breathing, or meditation techniques.

2 Secondary level (beliefs about self)

Q9 *What beliefs or values did you have that supported X?*

Addictive beliefs may have set up the system: 'I'm weak', 'I thought I didn't need people,' 'I believed I didn't have to face up to anything I didn't want to.'

Everyday beliefs about oneself keep the system going: 'I needed to enjoy life/fit in with other people/be creative/do my own thing,' etc.

Q10 *What beliefs/values do you have or may you rediscover to support change?*

Beliefs: client may be able to update beliefs they can see as out of date. Values: client to arrange in a hierarchy, identify if any need to be higher on the list to more effectively support change.

Q11 *Had you identified yourself with X? With being an X addict?*

There is frequently a struggle between 'core' self and addictive self. See Part IV on client issues for more about identification with X.

Q12 *What sense of yourself do you have that is more than your X behaviour/ feelings?*

"I am the sky and my emotions are the clouds," wrote T.S. Eliot. We can observe our shifting feelings and observe our changing behaviour. We can observe ourselves observing them. We can see X as an aspect of ourselves and not the whole. We can step outside ourselves to see what's going on.

3 Tertiary level (beliefs beyond self)

Jung reckoned that addictive behaviour is a distorted search for spiritual experience. Others believe that a spiritual deficit is responsible for the complete egocentricity displayed by some addicts.

Q13 *What is important to you beyond yourself? What is more important to you than that?*

A sense of community, spirituality, connectedness? Facilitator can continue asking the follow-up question until a core value / mission in life / place of belonging in the process of the universe is reached. The bigger picture, higher plane, or deeper level is unlikely to include X. The spiritual or communal component of some treatment programmes may be of benefit to addicts who have never connected to anything greater than themselves.

> I have been working with a middle-aged bachelor, Gerald, an habitual churchgoer until his mother died. Gerald is experiencing feelings of cruel desertion by God. He has given up attending church and has become addicted to therapy instead. It takes me a while to realize the extent of this dependency. As he talks about his doctor, psychiatrist, social worker, solicitor, physiotherapist, reflexologist, rheumatologist, solicitor, home help, and bereavement counsellor, I begin to realize that he hasn't seen all these people over the past year or two, but in the previous

fortnight. Gerald eventually generates a healing metaphor for his addiction to therapy. He calls it 'the love of God'. Not the establishment God – he is severely disillusioned with the standard version – but a more personal deity. He takes this healing metaphor to his overwhelming need for help and claims to be feeling better, but I'm not yet sure if he has swapped one set of dependencies for another.

Possession

Twelve questions about the nature of the client's attachment to the addiction.

Q14 *Has X helped you to avoid or evade something?*

Addiction almost always has its roots in the avoidance of something. It might be a terrible spectre of isolation and alienation; it might simply be feelings of loneliness or inadequacy.

Q15 *How may [the Q14 answer] be faced now to your benefit?*

Q16 *Has X sustained a special need for you? What has X wanted for you?*

There may be something unique to the client that was a means of giving the illusion of stability, support, security, specialness, power, etc.

Q17 *What other kinds of security/specialness/power are available or may be found that don't have the disadvantages of X? In what other ways may X's need for you be met?*

NLP's 6-step reframe [note 2, page 40] is a useful technique for helping someone who wants to change an old behaviour hold on to its benefits – being able to relax, express themselves, have a sense of belonging, etc. – while ridding themselves of its disbenefits.

Q18 *Has X helped your sense of belonging? Has X helped you separate from others?*

There is no assumption here that 'belonging' or 'separate' are desirable or undesirable, or that one state necessarily excludes the other. It depends entirely on the context and the circumstance.

Q19 *What more beneficial ways of belonging/separating are available to you or may you find?*

A 'perceptual positions' exercise will help the client appreciate a situation from the embodied point of view of associated others ... to take the learnings from that into the perception of an objective observer ... and to take the learnings from other and observer positions back into a newly embodied sense of self. Addicts are likely to be stuck in 1st (self) position; to find habitual rescuers or co-dependents in 2nd (other); and to find associates who deny any involvement in 3rd (observer). Finding a 4th ('meta-mirror') position allows the client to observe the relationship between self and observer as a reflection of the relationship between self and other, leading to the client considering, 'What can observer do to help self more?'

Q20 *Has X been a habit? How many X occasions were actually enjoyable?*

Many habitual smokers and drinkers hardly notice how much or when they consume. A habit may thus feed on itself, so that the behaviour becomes an inadvertent rule rather than a deliberate exception.

> In Irena's first session we go through a typical day – cigarette #1 on waking, #2 after breakfast, #3 walking to the station, etc. I ask her which is the least enjoyable. It is the first time she has considered the question. She realizes that the taste of the cigarette before breakfast is pretty awful. By our second session, she has cut this one out. She then calculates that only the first quarter of the cigarette after breakfast gives her what she wants. But it is not for another three weeks that the real reason Irena has come for counselling reveals itself: she is frightened of change. She realized this when she tried to stop smoking. She wants to stop only when it feels safe to stop. Safety and security are deeper issues for Irena than smoking. Her outcome evolves at the pace that is right for her.

Q21 *Was there another need we haven't identified that X met?*

If the pleasure associated with X has begun to fade, the client may be doing more X in an attempt to escape from the problem of diminishing returns.

And if loss of control or a very late stage of addiction is suspected:

Q22 *Have you blamed others for your X?*

Q23 *Have others withdrawn from you saying they had to protect themselves?*

Q24 *Have you lied about X in spite of promises to quit or cut down?*

Q25 *Has X been or become a ritual?*

A habit may only be at stage #3 or #4 of the Part II neurobiological model. A ritual is likely to be at stage #5, the stage before breakdown, though some addicts maintain themselves short of breakdown for years. It is at the ritual stage that alcoholics may be hiding bottles, anorexics secretly starving themselves, gamblers operating clandestine accounts, drug addicts stealing – rituals that weaken their links with others and strengthen their sense of possession by the object of the ritual.

Pattern

How have the client's life patterns related to unconscious patterns around the addiction? Five questions based on the structure and organization of their subjective experience.

> *The addiction is not the addictive substance, it is not even the particular sensations, perceptions, behaviours, and beliefs experienced by the addict, it is the organization of the relationships between those experiences which mean the pattern repeats over and over.*
> Penny Tompkins and James Lawley

Q26 *Has it seemed as if a bad feeling gave rise to your desire to/for X?*

The emotional → physical connective pattern. A few clients will have enough insight into themselves and their behaviour to be able to acknowledge these bodymind signals. As they learn to 'listen to their bodies' for information, they have to learn to interpret what they hear. A once-addictive bodymind in recovery is making constant adjustments to radically different patterns and conditions, and might easily mistake an uncomfortable feeling related to normal stress as a craving for X. The client may need to stop and ask themself basic questions: Am I in fact hungry? Angry? Frustrated? Tired?

Q27 *Or has doing X seemed to make you feel good?*

The physical → emotional pattern. See the Part II model. Many substance-dependent clients perceive their addiction this way. They may not have the insight to make the emotional → physical connection, or it might be simple conditioning: physical event associated with pleasurable situation prompts learned response in the brain. It may only be a certain cue in the situation that gives the high. Inhaling cigarette smoke may be the only time the client breathes fully (+ive state). Chocolate often has strong cultural associations with gifts or treats (+ive state). Alcohol or coffee may be associated with socializing (+ve state). The addict learns to identify X with a high for which credit is due elsewhere. Changing the pattern means separating out information going into the brain in such a way that an existing unwanted pattern is not reinforced.

Q28 *What has been the sequence of events that linked your (+ve or –ve) state of mind to X? How specifically were you making the link?*

I have not yet met a client yet who with attentive support could not 'freeze frame' a typical moment and analyse their hitherto unconscious strategy around it: what led up to that moment and what happened just after it? It is one of the areas in which Clean Language questioning comes into its own. "What happens *just* before?" "And *then* what happens?"

Q29 *How may you make a more beneficial connection?*

There are at least five possible places to intervene in a typical addictive sequence in terms of the Part II model: (1) at the link between trigger event and associated feeling; (2) at the link between feeling and judgment of feeling; (3) at the link between judgment of feeling and associated bodymind state; (4) at the link between associated bodymind state and desire for X; and (5) at the link between desire for X and doing X.

(1) Trigger event / → / Associated feeling
(2) Feeling / → / Judgment of feeling
(3) Judgment of feeling / → / Bodymind state
(4) Bodymind state / → / Desire for X
(5) Desire for X / → / Doing X

Whichever key stage the client is aware of first (event, feeling, judgment, bodymind state, desire for X) can be expanded in spacetime and explored to create an alternative link that results in a different behaviour. Clearly, the earlier in the sequence that the new behaviour is triggered, the more effective the trickle-down effect is likely to be.

Clean questioning is not the only way of making time and space at the junction between one event and the next. Relaxation, visualization, and breathing techniques can be employed so that old connections are not triggered anew. The five-stage progression may be habitual, but is not immutable.

> Jane is a 28-year old actor possessed by anger. If something goes badly wrong for her, she explodes emotionally. When she analyses her unconsciously constructed strategy for anger, it goes something like this: outside event (e.g. being interrupted while talking) → internal bad feeling → irritation → physical tremors → frustration → anger → verbal/physical explosion. At one point while she is talking, I interrupt and ask her to access a mild version of her anger. She does so. I invite her to explore the physical tremors she is experiencing. She stands up and walks around.
>
> The tremors seem to centre on her right foot. She says, "I feel just like stamping my foot and going 'Poo!'" She laughs. She is embarrassed. Suddenly, she has a memory of herself as a three- or four-year old, being restrained by her mother in a shop when all she wants to do is run off and look at toys. With her little right foot she stamps on her mother's foot in a moment of pique. Adult Jane is dismayed at the memory, but having deconstructed it, goes on to build a new sequence using the feeling in her foot as a cue to

'step back' in potentially frustrating situations and re-assess. The direct, unconscious link with anger is broken.

The brain is a selective recognition system. It learns to sensitize itself to particular stimuli from the outside world, so that when present events remind us of similar events in the past, we have ready-made ways of responding. Unfortunately, the brain doesn't always distinguish whether learned responses are appropriate to present needs. The more information we have about our habitual patterns for processing information and acting on it, the better we can construct and implement new strategies.

Q30 *What position in the family were you? What was your experience of that? How might that have contributed to your strengths? To your vulnerabilities? What do you learn from that?*

A few generalizations: first-borns may experience expectations of high achievement and become workaholics; middle children drawn to peer groups may become involved in drug abuse; last children if loners may seek sexual promiscuity as a substitute for love, or if over-protected may be prone to anxiety and phobias. Family patterns of expectation and reaction will affect adult patterns of addiction and recovery.

Q31 *Do you want to make your own choices about how you quit or control X or do you prefer having external rules to follow?*

Rule followers dependent on external authority almost certainly need to develop a sense of internal authority (which may or may not include self-generated rules). There are plenty of addiction programmes – behavioural techniques and twelve-step rituals – for rule followers. Own-choice clients may simply want support to help them make their choices.

> I believe that Brian (drinking and depression), is getting somewhere in his therapy when he corrects me for the first time. It is his fifth session and I have fallen into the trap of thinking I know him. I venture a glib interpretation of some behaviour. "No, it's not like that!" he blurts out. He blushes. He apologises. It is the first time Brian has not been a 'good client'. Years ago, he had learnt to be a 'good son' to appease an abusive father, who not surprisingly had a drinking problem himself. Brian went on to became a 'good pupil' who did not do well at school; a 'good friend' who was unable to sustain a relationship for very long; and a 'good worker' who eventually got the sack because of his alcoholism.
>
> I could probably have provoked Brian into disagreeing with me earlier (though that may be me wanting to be 'good therapist'), but

from the moment he stops deferring to me and listens to his own voice, he begins to make progress.

Preference

Addiction can seem to mean having no choice. Here are five questions exploring the possibilities and pitfalls of choice. For some addicts, a basic change would mean knowing that there *is* choice. The questions in this frame try not to presuppose a 'right' choice. This is an activating-for-change, not a directionalizing-for-change, model. A client still has to do what a client has to do in a way and at a pace that is right for them. The questions presuppose only that the client wishes to do something about X. Note that these are not simple choices.

Q32 *Are you ready to change? Can you choose to X or not-X each time?*

Every day something happens with the potential to precipitate a former dependency. Sitting down to eat. Walking past a favourite pub. The mere fact of an infinite number of choices between X (addiction) and not-X (abstinence) polarities may explain why some ex-addicts find it easy to slip back into addiction. They make small midpoint choices – smoking only at weekends, confining themselves to three cups of coffee a day – and hope to stick at that. It can work. Total abstinence-based programmes report high failure rates. But an excess of choice can be confusing and anxiety-inducing, like having to pick your way through a minefield. A way out of this paradox – if polarities have an infinite number of midpoint possibilities between them, how can total addiction or total abstinence exist at all? – is not to avoid responsibility and allow external events to dictate our behaviour, but to recognize our personal thresholds: our sense of the X or not-X threshold choices that uniquely predispose us towards one hypothetical endpoint or the other. The question then becomes: where do we wish to be on the X / not-X continuum and what needs to happen to achieve that?

Q33 *Do you wish to fully expand your choices to include the possibility of X behaviour? Or to limit your choices only to not-X behaviour?*

A client may need to prove to themself that they can resist X before being ready to choose between X and not-X. And these X and not-X choices have to be taken every time.

Q34 *Can you choose to avoid any desire for X and risk it being triggered unexpectedly? Or to allow the desire without thinking you have to act on it?*

The state of unease associated with choice is known to us all. For some people, having a choice means having to choose, which they can only do if they know the 'right' choice first. Whereas having choice is simply that: it confers freedom, because *it does not have to be chosen*. And if you happen to believe that the act of choosing results in the removal of choice: come off it, there are always more choices!

Q35 *Will you choose the temporary discomforts of desire over the permanent discomforts of possession?*

The question accepts that one of these states has to take precedence over the other in a situation where a person cannot exist in both. It also acknowledges the unlikelihood of achieving the resolution of all underlying, unresolved need overnight and contains the barest of hints that desire may be a preferable hassle (as a state that waxes and wanes) to possession (which is likely to be continual disaster). The facilitator can accompany the client on a walk down two imaginary timelines into the future to help them access and explore these alternatives as if they were contemporary states. It will help clarify the advantages and disadvantages of either choice. And it is, finally, a choice.

The last question may also (in Clean Language terms at least) be the first and may be asked at any point of departure in-between. It is totally self-reflective:

Q36 *And now what do you know?*

The answer can be at any level of the client's perception.

It may or may not be a coincidence that the number thirty-six is the sum of a full Emergent Knowledge therapeutic procedure – an algorithm of six rounds of six iterative questions. Q36 could itself signal the start of such a specialized process.[1]

The expansion of self-information that results from this activating-for-change questionnaire will serve to dispel anxiety, resolve duality, and facilitate a move to whatever variation of non-addiction, compulsion, or dependency the client can achieve. The expectation of this epic journey is that the persistent stress of possession will cede power and presence to the occasional, bearable, almost certainly preferable discomforts of desire. It's not cool to be an addict. At best, you are a nuisance. At worst, it will kill you.

© 2012 Philip Harland

Note to Part VI

[1] *Emergent Knowledge process*: for a full explanation, see *The Power of Six: A Six Part Guide to Self Knowledge* (Wayfinder 2009, 2012).

Philip Harland is a psychotherapist who worked in analytic, humanistic, and neurolinguistic therapies before specializing in Clean Language, Therapeutic Metaphor, and Emergent Knowledge. He is the author of *Trust Me, I'm The Patient: Clean Language, Metaphor, and the New Psychology of Change.*

Acknowledgments

Penny Tompkins, James Lawley, and Carol Thompson for their constructive suggestions and attention to detail. Earlier versions of the articles that make up this paper appeared in Rapport, the quarterly journal of the UK Association for NLP, and at cleanlanguage.co.uk

References and Further Reading

Pamela Gawler-Wright, Working Successfully with Addictions seminars
Doug Thorburn, Alcoholism Myths and Realities, Galt Publishing 2005
Maureen Canning: Lust, Anger, Love: Understanding Sexual Addiction, 2008
Bruce K. Alexander, The Globalization of Addiction, Addiction Research 8, 2000
John R Searle, The Rediscovery of the Mind, MIT Press 1994; Mind, Language and Society, Weidenfeld and Nicholson 1999
Gerald Edelman, Bright Air, Brilliant Fire: On the Matter of the Mind, Allen Lane 1992
Anne Wilson Schaef, Beyond Therapy, Beyond Science, HarperSanFrancisco 1992
John Firman and Ann Gila, The Primal Wound, a Transpersonal View of Trauma, Addiction and Growth, State University of New York Press 1997
Craig Nakken, Addictive Personality: Roots, Ritual and Recovery, Hazelden 1996
Chelly M. Sterman, ed. Neuro-Linguistic Programming in Alcoholism Treatment, Haworth Press 1990
Mara Selvini Palazzoli et al, Paradox and Counter-Paradox, Jason Aranson Inc.
Ian McDermott and Joseph O'Connor, NLP and Health, Thorsons 1996
Sid Jacobson, A Summary of Important Considerations in Quitting or Controlling Smoking, South Central Institute of NLP, USA
Tina Stacey, Addiction and the 12-State Steps, seminar and personal communication
James Lawley and Penny Tompkins, Metaphors in Mind: Transformation through Symbolic Modelling, Developing Company Press 2000

Self-Help Groups

Addictions Anonymous, Adult Children of Alcoholics, Al-Anon, Alcoholics Anonymous, Cocaine Anonymous, Co-dependents Anonymous, Council for Involuntary Tranquilizer Addiction, Debtors Anonymous, Emotions Anonymous, Gamblers Anonymous, Helpers Anonymous, Narcotics Anonymous, Overeaters Anonymous, Pills Anonymous, Secular Organization for Sobriety, Sex Addicts Anonymous, Sexual Compulsives Anonymous, Workaholics Anonymous, and others.

Notes

Appendix
Checklist for Change

Everyone has to progress through an extensive self-reflective sequence before change will be secured and maintained. This checklist can be used alongside the Information Activating and Change questionnaire.

There are at least twenty separate but intimately related incremental changes for the bodymind to make before unaddicting can take full effect:

1. naming X (the unwanted addiction, pattern or behaviour) →
2. acknowledging it rather than denying its reality →
3. accepting rather than hating it →
4. appreciating it for having had an honourable intention →
5. thanking it for its attempts to secure that intention →
6. loving it for its part in the survival of the whole →
7. loving the whole for accommodating X →
8. understanding that X is now out of date →
9. discovering X's underlying need for the whole

If step #9 reveals a hitherto unacknowledged addiction underlying X, return to step #1. If not, continue to →

10. desiring to bring the whole up-to-date →
11. allowing support on the road to self-reliance →
12. being willing to change beliefs and behaviour to that end →
13. intending to change

An accumulation of each of these critical transitions must be experienced in order to support the crucial →

14. deciding to change →
15. committing to change →
16. facing the possibility of reality and pain →
17. learning new life skills →
18. monitoring the change →
19. testing it →
20. maintaining it.

Those who work their way (with support) through this sequence are not merely ridding themselves of an unwanted addiction, but improving their lives as a whole.

www.ingramcontent.com/pod-product-compliance
Ingram Content Group UK Ltd.
Pitfield, Milton Keynes, MK11 3LW, UK
UKHW041959230426
12048UKWH00008B/414